BASEBALL
BY THE BEACH

BASEBALL
BY THE BEACH

A HISTORY OF AMERICA'S NATIONAL
PASTIME ON CAPE COD

Christopher Price

On Cape Publications

Yarmouth Port, Massachusetts

For my parents.

Contents

Acknowledgments

You very rarely get a second chance to do anything in life, but I was lucky enough to get another printing of the book you are holding in your hands. I would like to reiterate my appreciation to all those who helped me with the initial printing--whether friend, co-worker or boss--you all played a big role in helping the original project reach fruition.

But this printing was a long time in coming, and there were several people who made it possible, not the least of which was Adam Gamble of On Cape Publications. He took a book that was dead in the water and helped to bring it back to life.

There were several friends, roommates and co-workers along the way who gave encouragement--and bought tons of copies of the first printing--who weren't mentioned in the first book. Julie Cornell provided support, a sturdy car to help provide transportation, and a kick in the pants to tell me it was time to revisit this project. Good friends and co-workers like Heidi Guarino, Jennifer Lefferts, Jay Rizoli and Andrew Bryce, as well as the entire staff at the Taunton Gazette, SchoolSports and Boston Metro. You have all provided support and laughter along the way.

Each and every one of the teams that sells the book at their souvenir stands also deserve big thanks, especially the folks in Wareham, Chatham, Brewster and Orleans. The first year the book was out, I discovered that the people who toil long hours at the concession stands dishing out hot dogs or who spend the game making popcorn are sometimes just as important as the star players and coaches.

And ultimately, my wife, Kate. There would be no new edition without her. As the wife of a sportswriter, she puts up with more long hours, frequent road trips and constant griping about sports than any woman ever should. Thank you.

Introduction
"Baseball Like It Oughta Be"

In 1986, the New York Mets' motto was "Baseball like it oughta be!" With their strutting, preening and excessive braggadocio, it was evident to any baseball fan outside of Queens that this wasn't baseball like it oughta be. But, the Cape Cod Baseball League really *is* baseball like it oughta be.

The game is played from June through August in the wide-open, lush fields of Yarmouth and in the shadow of an old brick schoolhouse in Hyannis. It's played in the thick woods of Harwich, in front of the loyal and loving crowds of Orleans, and in the fog and salt air of Chatham.

But for over 100 years, it has been enough that the game itself is actually played. The teams, the towns and players change from year to year, but the game has stayed the same since it was first introduced to Cape Cod in the mid-1800s. And that is enough to bring fans, scouts, players and tourists from around the country to witness what could be the last surviving form of pure and innocent baseball left in this country.

Baseball is often celebrated as an intra-generational game, and that has never been more true than here on Cape Cod. To understand baseball on the Cape, it is important to know that the grandparents of the man who owns the Barnstable Bat Company housed the entire Hyannis town team for the 1932 and 1933 seasons. It is important to know that Ted Rose played in the league thirty summers after his father, Glenn Rose, played in the league.

The list of today's major leaguers who have played on the Cape reads like an all-star roll call. Frank Thomas, Jeff Bagwell, Will Clark, Albert Belle, Mo Vaughn, Chuck Knoblauch, Ben McDonald, Terry Steinbach, Tim Salmon, Hal Morris, Chris Sabo, Mickey Tettleton, Walt Weiss, Robin Ventura, Charles Nagy, Kirk McCaskill and Scott Erickson have all played in the league since 1980.

But the list of retired greats touches almost every end of the baseball world, reaching all the way back to the '20s and '30s. It covers a country in the throes of a Depression, two World Wars and continues up to the modern computer age. Mickey Cochrane, Pie Traynor, Carlton Fisk, Thurman Munson, Charlie Hough and Mike Flanagan all played on the Cape at one time or another.

It is also a breeding ground for managers and front office people. Future managers such as Buck Showalter (Arizona Diamondbacks), Jim Riggleman (Chicago Cubs), and Bobby Valentine (New York Mets), as well as general managers such as Brian Sabean (San Francisco), Tom Grieve (former Texas GM, current Rangers broadcaster) and other key front office personnel such as Bill Livesey (Director of Scouting, Tampa Bay Devil Rays) and Bob Schaefer (Director of Minor League Field Operations for the Boston Red Sox) all played or managed on the Cape.

Among its prestigious alumni, there are five American League Rookies of the Year, two National League Rookies of the Year, two AL MVP's, one NL MVP, and two AL Cy Young Award winners.

Of the total number who played in the Major Leagues in 1994, 102 players had Cape League experience. Thirty-seven of them toiled in the National League and 65 of them played in the American League. Approximately one in every eight major leaguers has had Cape League experience. A good example of the Cape League's far-reaching pool of talent was the 1995 Major League All-Star Game. Eleven of the 56 All-Stars selected by the fans and the managers had Cape League experience, including some of the most exciting young stars in the game.

Frank Thomas, Erik Hanson and Jeff Conine (Orleans), Mo Vaughn (Wareham), Tyler Greene (Hyannis), Albert Belle (Hyannis and Chatham), Kevin Seitzer (Chatham), Tino Martinez (Fal-

Managing the Hyannis Mets in the 1970s was the first step on a
long baseball career for Bob Schaefer. After the Cape League,
he would work with the Yankees, Mets, Tigers and Royals in
several capacities. He is currently the Director of
Field Operations for the Red Sox minor leagues.
Photo courtesy Jack Aylmer.

mouth) and Dennis Neagle, Craig Biggio and Mickey Morandini (Yarmouth-Dennis) were all considered the best in the game that year, and all played at least one season in the Cape League. In addition, American League manager Buck Showalter (Hyannis) and AL coach Brian Butterfield (Wareham) had played in the CCBL.

"The Cape League is one of the best amateur leagues that we have in the game today," says New York Yankees pitching coach Mel Stottlemyre, whose two sons played in the Cape League in the 1980s. "They get the better college players, players that are going to have a chance to play professional baseball. They also play with the wood bats, something that a lot of the hitters experience for the first time. I think it's a real good league, and would recommend it to anyone."

"The Cape Cod League is a darned good league," says Boston Red Sox coach Johnny Pesky. "It's great for the guys that have a chance to play ball, and a lot of scouts go down and watch that league, and rightfully so. They do a great job. I know if I was a baseball fan and if I lived on that side of Boston I'd be down there all the time."

"I know it's always been a good league," said former Colorado Silver Bullets manager Phil Niekro after a 1996 exhibition between the Silver Bullets and a collection of Cape League All-Stars. "There is a history of great players who have been here. But one thing that has really impressed me is the people that surround the league. The hospitality, the host families that took our players. This is one of the highlights for us that will always stand out for all of us."

And it's not just professional baseball. Six of the players on the 1996 U.S. Olympic baseball team were former Cape Leaguers, including star pitchers such as Kris Benson (Hyannis) and Braden Looper (Cotuit).

Ironically, it is the New York Yankees who, for many years, seemed to be the fondest of Cape League alumni. The Yankees, traditionally despised throughout New England, have a long history of snatching some of the best players and coaches the CCBL has to offer. The list includes former managers such as Showalter and Stump Merrill, coaches such as Butterfield and former Yan-

Not all of the ballplayers who performed in the Cape League
went on to become famous on the diamond. Bill Richardson
was a hard-throwing right-hander who pitched for Harwich
in 1966 and Cotuit in 1967. He went on to serve in
Congress, as well as the United States Ambassador
to the United Nations.

**Kris Benson, 1996 Olympian and first pick in the 1996 amateur draft, spent a summer with the Hyannis Mets.
Photo courtesy Jack Aylmer.**

kees bullpen catcher Glenn Sherlock (who played for Yarmouth-Dennis), scouts like Livesey (who has been affiliated with five different Cape organizations as a player and a coach before becoming the chief scout for the Yankees and the Devil Rays), Pat Sullivan (who played for Wareham) and Paul Turco (who played for Falmouth). Many of these same coaches and scouts have since moved on to join Showalter with the Diamondbacks, who began play in 1998.

"You get a lot of coaches in college baseball who have played here," says John Claffey, who has been associated with the league for 20 years. "There was a coach we had in Hyannis one year, Glen Tufts. He's with the Giants now, and he's coaching at the Single A level. He's been here, and knows what it is like. With the Yankees, there was Livesey and Gillis, who was Livesey's number one right-hand man. At one point there were eight people in the Yankees management system who played in the Cape Cod League."

But it is Bill Livesey, perhaps more than any other, who is responsible for getting the Cape League name circulated throughout the baseball underground.

"The proliferation of scouts throughout Major League Baseball who have Cape League experience has happened because of Bill Livesey," says Jack Aylmer, a Cape League historian who has been responsible for getting three separate franchises off the ground. "It has also happened because of Bob Schaefer, who was with the Yankee organization and is now in charge of Red Sox player development."

But while players are more often than not transients passing through, happy to spend a couple of months playing baseball in a summer vacation area, it is the league's staff and the many volunteers who truly make the league the success that it is. Judy Scarafile, Arnold Mycock and William J. Lovell are just some of the people who have contributed to the success of the CCBL.

"It's the organization of the volunteers that makes the Cape League special," says former Seattle Mariners scout Jack Webber. "They have very dedicated people in the community, who do everything from making sandwiches after the game, to manicuring

The Cape Cod Baseball League is one of the few places that young baseball fans can get close to their heroes. Photo courtesy Judy Scarafile.

the field, to getting the kids jobs and housing. It's a special place because of those people."

"The Cape Cod League is like a Broadway musical," says John Claffey, who has been associated with the league in various capacities for close to 20 years. "The players are the stars. Everyone else is like a stagehand, pulling the curtain up and down."

"You have the best of both worlds," says Mo Vaughn, first baseman for the Boston Red Sox. He played for Wareham in 1988, on what many consider one of the finest Cape teams ever. "You have great baseball, and a great atmosphere at the same time."

"There's something special about going over the bridge and onto the Cape, especially in the summertime," says former Cape League Umpire-in-Chief Nick Zibelli. "It's like going into another world, a fantasy land of baseball. Each one of the little villages is so involved in the game of baseball."

"It's the best organized nonprofessional league I've seen," asserts former Boston Red Sox scout Bill Enos.

"It's a great summer for the people who are spectators," according to ESPN baseball analyst Peter Gammons. "And it's the best summer on earth for the guys who play there."

But it is the relationship between the players and the fans that quite often makes the best stories. The spectators get the opportunity to see a player when he is still early in his career, learning the intricacies of the game. And the player not only makes a fan for life, he quite often makes a friend, thus humanizing the game . . . and making it baseball as it oughta be!

PART I

From Town Teams
to League Play:
1840–1962

· 1 ·

The Massachusetts Game

"Baseball is one of the few things still left that ties communities together, and when you look at the Cape Cod Baseball League, the area is already such a wonderful community, the league becomes a symbol of that group of people. I think it represents the wonderful people of the Cape."
—Ken Burns, Creator of the PBS program "Baseball."

To find the true origins of the game of baseball on Cape Cod, one must first look at the history of the game itself. No one is sure of the specific date when the first baseball game was played, but we do know that a version of the game, of which today's modern game is a direct descendant, was invented in New York in the mid-1840s and was originally called "base," "stool ball," "one-old-cat" or "bat-and-ball," a derivation of what many believe to be the British game of rounders or cricket. The game began sweeping the nation throughout the 1840s and 1850s.

"In our sun-down perambulations of late, through the outer parts of Brooklyn, we have observed several parties of youngsters playing 'base,' a certain game of ball," poet Walt Whitman wrote in 1846. "Let us go forth awhile, and get better air in our lungs. Let us leave our close rooms. The game of ball is glorious."

"Like everything else American, it came with a rush," noted John Montgomery Ward, a star player of the era. "The game is

1

suited to the national temperament. It requires strength, courage and skill; it is full of dash and excitement and though a most difficult game in which to excel, it is yet extremely simple in its first principles and easily understood by everyone."

The Civil War did much to spread the game throughout the country. Veterans returning home from the war would tell tales of this new game, and its popularity continued to spread. Many believe this is how the game arrived in southeastern Massachusetts.

"The parade ground has been a busy place for a week or so past, ball-playing having become a mania in camp," wrote Private Alpherus B. Parker of the 10th Massachusetts Regiment on April 21, 1863. "Officers and men forget, for a time, their differences in rank and indulge in the invigorating sport with a schoolboy's ardor."

And when the game began to spread, different variations of the fledgling sport took hold in different parts of the country. Warren Goldstein reveals in *Playing for Keeps: A History of Early Baseball* that a version of baseball called the "Massachusetts game" (also referred to as "Boston Ball") differed from the more popular and standard version of the game that first arose in the New York/New Jersey area.

"Differing from the New York game in several particulars," Goldstein noted, "the bases were laid out in a square rather than a diamond, an inning was over when just one batter was put out, and the winner was the first side to score 100 runs—the Massachusetts game dominated New England baseball until the early 1860s, when a number of older clubs switched their allegiances and new clubs were formed to play what had become known by then as the 'National Association game.'"

But the Massachusetts game was the object of much scorn among newfound baseball purists. Author and historian John Thorn wrote in *Baseball: Our Game* that the Massachusetts game resembled the old English game rounders, a less "manly" version of baseball, and therefore it was the object of derision.

"What brought scorn upon the heads of these staunch devotees of town ball (also known as "Boston Ball" or the "Massachusetts Game") was that although the game had regularly positioned fielders and demanded a modicum of strategic play, it still bore the childish essence of rounders: the retirement of a baserunner by throwing the ball at him, which necessitated a softer, less resilient ball than that used in the manly sport of cricket," Thorn writes.

But in the 19th century many people throughout the country flocked to baseball games with great frequency. The game was played mainly in country parks, but with America's movement from an agrarian nation to an industrial one, the game began to catch on in the cities as well. Leagues sprang up overnight, and seemingly disappeared just as quickly.

Organized sports of any kind didn't reach Cape Cod until the mid-19th century. Prior to this, settlers had little time for sports. Competition in the 18th century centered around hunting or fishing, with target shooting often the sport of choice. According to one historian, the Native Americans played a form of football "on wide, sandy beaches." Bowling, dice and cards were widely played, except on the Sabbath.

In the latter half of the 19th century, horseracing became popular. Harwich's Wychmere Harbor saw many exciting races, as did the Hyannis Trotting Park in Barnstable. One of the first trots at Hyannis was held on July 4, 1876 and attracted 300 carriages and 1,200 spectators, while another meet in August drew 2,000 onlookers. As a result of the immense popularity of horse racing, nearly all the villages of Barnstable had trotting parks. Golf courses sprung up on the Cape in the 1890s in Hyannis and Cummaquid, and tourists flocked to the game in large numbers.

By the late 19th century, baseball was known throughout the Cape. Historian James Ellis revealed in the summer 1981 issue of *Cape Cod Life* that Civil War veterans recalled in an 1867 issue of the *Barnstable Patriot* that baseball was a new and curious sport. One player liked the game even though the pitcher "sent 'em in hot. Hot balls in time of war are good. But I don't like 'em too hot for fun." Another observer noted "It is the most radical play I know of, this base ball." He continued to make a rather bizarre analogy, saying that "Sawing cordwood is moonlight rambles besides base ball." Nonetheless, baseball was taking hold on the Cape.

For years, the Cape Cod Baseball League has promoted 1885

as its starting date for organized play on the Cape. As evidence, they point as proof of the league's true age to a faded publicity poster now hanging at the Baseball Hall of Fame in Cooperstown, New York, that promotes a July 4th game between Barnstable and Sandwich. However, this point has been open to debate for many years. Records indicate that the 1885 game may indeed have been the 12th annual contest on the Cape itself. On Election Day, November 7, 1865, according to the *Barnstable Patriot*, the Cummaquids of Barnstable beat the Mastetuketts of West Barnstable.

Many of those players from the Mastetuketts of West Barnstable would later constitute the first organized baseball team on the Cape. Called the Nichols Baseball Club of Sandwich, they were formally established in June of 1866, and named after a retired sea captain who was the only farmer in Sandwich to allow the club to play on his land.

The *Barnstable Patriot* also noted that Sandwich was quickly becoming a baseball town. As early as August 13, 1867, the newspaper noted that a second team from Sandwich hosted a visiting Cummaquid team from West Barnstable.

Most of these games were played between towns simply for the joy of competition. But in September of 1867, the Cummaquid Club of Barnstable and the Mattakeesetts of Yarmouth played one another at the Annual Cattle Show and Fair with a little more on the line. Cummaquid won 30–13, taking home the trophy. "The prize . . . was a beautiful silver-mounted carved walnut bat costing $15," reported the *Patriot*.

Baseball fever began to sweep the Cape, but for a variety of reasons not all the aspiring teams could afford to keep up with the pace. In August of 1868, a *Barnstable Patriot* story reported: "On Friday night this week, the store of Elva Hallway was robbed of a number of baseballs, by a window removed. A new club will probably be started."

By the 1880s, baseball was well entrenched as a popular Cape Cod pastime, thanks in part to a New Englander who would soon call Cape Cod home. Dickey Pearce was at the forefront of the game in the late 19th century and is credited with several innova-

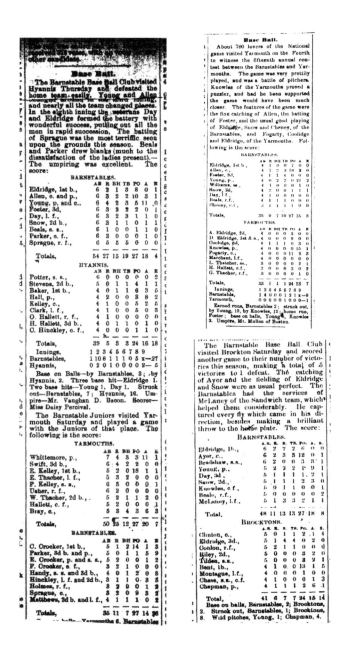

Early accounts of baseball on Cape Cod, as printed in the pages of the *Barnstable Patriot*, seem to contradict the league's assertion that the CCBL began in 1885. Reproduction courtesy of the *Barnstable Patriot*.

tions, including inventing the bunt and modernizing the position of shortstop.

According to many, Pearce invented the "fair/foul" hit (also known as the "tricky hit") in the mid-1870s, whereby the hitter would deaden the ball and push it to the left side of the plate (considered a "drag bunt" today). After starting fair, the ball would roll foul, making it a legal hit and impossible for an infielder to throw the hitter out. Reports said it took the baseball world by storm, with one account telling about a hit going over the catcher's head and over the backstop for a homer.

Pearce was also a pioneer defensively. He started playing professionally in 1856, when the position of shortstop was different, with the fielder rarely moving from the area between second and third. But the stocky Pearce changed all that, playing himself according to the hitters, shifting one way or another when needed. His pudgy frame didn't allow for much speed, but he compensated for that limitation by using judgment and anticipation.

Soon after his professional retirement he moved to Cape Cod, where he lived as a celebrity, often making appearances at Old-Timers Games. In 1908, he caught a flu bug at an Old Timers Game in Boston. The illness was serious enough to confine the 72-year-old Pearce to his bed in Wareham, where he later died. But even in death, his legend grew. A 1911 story in the *New York Journal* by sportswriter Sam Crane ranked him eighth on a list of the 50 greatest ballplayers in history.

Baseball historian Dick Thompson would also discover other Cape natives who toiled in the major leagues in the late 19th century and the early 20th century. The Providence club of 1884 featured a pitcher named Ed Conley and listed his birthplace as Chicago. However, Thompson traced his birth to Sandwich, in 1864. Conley finished the 1884 campaign with a 4–4 record, and all his starts were complete games. (Even more impressive that year was the performance of Conley's teammate, Old Hoss Radburn. Radburn threw an amazing 679 innings over the season, posting a 60–12 record.) Thompson also found Joel Sherman, who was born in Yarmouth in 1890 and threw twice for the Philadel-

Dickey Pearce

Dickey Pearce, one of the lesser known heroes of baseball's early days, started playing professionally in 1856 and is credited as the inventor of the bunt, as well as being the man who defensively modernized the position of shortstop. Pearce died in 1908, and is buried in Onset. Photo courtesy Baseball Hall of Fame.

phia Athletics. He retired undefeated with a career mark of 1–0 while later playing for the legendary Connie Mack.

Interestingly, Thompson also discovered that many former major leaguers chose the Cape as their final resting place. George Moore, who pitched for the Pittsburgh Pirates in 1905, died in Hyannis on November 4, 1948. Foster Edwards who played for the Boston Braves and the New York Giants in the late ´20s with a 6–9 mound mark expired in Orleans on January 4, 1980. Dave Morey of the 1913 Philadelphia Athletics passed away on Martha's Vineyard, and Wild Bill Hunnefield, White Sox shortstop in the ´20s, died on Nantucket.

In 1883, the Barnstable Village team claimed the southeastern Massachusetts championship after beating Middleboro, 24–8. Throughout the late 19th century, almost every town on the Cape began to organize teams to meet in a loosely designated championship tournament, held each fall at the Barnstable County Agricultural Fair.

Baseball exploded in popularity throughout the country in the early 1900s. From 1901 through 1909, the American and National League counted over 7.2 million paying customers who had streamed through the turnstiles. Many feel that the growth of the game was tied directly to the rise of the American city. In 1900, 40 percent of all Americans lived in the city. Just 10 years later, that number had risen to 46 percent. By 1920, it was up to 50 percent and still growing. Urban dwellers were looking for something to occupy their leisure time. Baseball filled the bill.

To satisfy their customers, owners were building palatial new ballparks. From 1909 through 1913, six vintage ballparks opened their gates to the public: Fenway Park in Boston, Comiskey Park in Chicago, Shibe Park in Philadelphia, Forbes Field in Pittsburgh, and the Polo Grounds and Ebbetts Field in New York. To keep Cape Cod's baseball fans up to date, the local newspapers began publishing boxscores and extensive game stories in the early 20th century. In fact, the game was becoming so popular that larger towns began fielding two teams. In 1909, Barnstable had two teams, one of them playing at Hallett's Field and another at the corner of North and Winter Streets in Hyannis.

"In those day, even more so than today, every young boy on the Cape played baseball," said Tod Owen, who played on a Falmouth team in the early days of the 20th century. "We didn't have the competition from soccer and basketball and hockey that they have today. So baseball was a bigger thing in the life of a youth in those days than it is now."

The development of baseball continued through the efforts of the Cape League in the early decades of the 20th century. In the years prior to World War I, many semipro teams came on the scene, and financing became a problem. To circumvent these difficulties, many teams began charging admission. In 1909, Barnstable sold tickets that cost 15 cents for women and 20 cents for men. In 1917, Hyannis sold season tickets for "2$ (*sic*) transferable, with ladies admitted free."

Transportation to and from the games was also a problem. Cars were still relatively new, so many players hopped trains and would often be on them the entire day if they were traveling from one end of the Cape to the other.

"In those early days, it took us all day to get to games," Owen said. "It took us all day to get to Chatham from Falmouth. The roads were narrow, and most of them were just country roads. You'd get in the middle of town, and you'd have to go slowly. Mostly, we traveled around by buckboards. Some had individual cars. Some took the trains. It was quite a trip to come from Falmouth to Orleans."

In 1918, the Falmouth town team underwent a change. Unable to afford to field a team, they merged with Oak Bluffs of Martha's Vineyard. When in Falmouth, it was "strictly a Falmouth team," noted the *Brockton Enterprise*. "The players wear our uniform . . . In Oak Bluffs they are the Vineyard's team."

In the early 1920s, teams from all parts of southeastern Massachusetts regularly faced the Cape's semipro clubs. Teams from Boston, Bridgewater, Brockton, Canton, Fairhaven, Hull, Middleboro, New Bedford, Plymouth, Taunton and Weymouth often visited the Cape during the summer and fall to provide competition. It was one of these visits from a southeastern Massachusetts team that may have caused the Cape League to select the legendary Mickey Cochrane as one of their own.

One of the most disputed facts in the long history of the Cape League is whether or not Cochrane actually played on the Cape. He was one of the greatest catchers of all time, but he was a shortstop when it is claimed that his team visited Cape Cod in the early 1920s.

Born and raised in Bridgewater, Massachusetts, Cochrane played five varsity sports while an undergraduate at Boston University. Documents reveal that, during the summer, he played semipro ball under the name "Frank King" in order to keep his eligibility at B.U. It was commonplace for players of the day to do such things, but it has made attempts to verify his appearance in the Cape League difficult, at best.

However, Barnstable historian James Ellis uncovered a Frank King who had played for Dover of the Eastern Shore League in 1923. While a further search has failed to uncover a Frank King (or even a Cochrane) playing for any Cape League team, a "King" (first name unknown) did play shortstop for Middleboro in 1920. At that time, Cochrane was playing as an infielder. Apparently, this is enough evidence for the league to claim Cochrane as one of their own, despite many opinions to the contrary.

Nicknamed "Black Mike" for the dark moods he would sink into after his teams lost, Cochrane would post a career batting average of .320 over a 13-year career in the majors. Based on his career with Philadelphia and Detroit, he was inducted into the Hall of Fame in 1947.

"At that time, all the big Cape hotels had teams, but they weren't as formidable as the other club teams," Owen recalled. "We were never lacking for places to go or teams to play."

Unfortunately, all of this competition cost money: approximately $170 a game to provide transportation, equipment and the like. As a result, the Barnstable Agricultural Society decided to limit County Fair baseball tournaments to Cape teams only, beginning in 1921, "to generate more local interest."

The Cape baseball championship would be determined each fall at the fair, perhaps the largest single annual gathering in southeastern Massachusetts. Falmouth took the title in 1921 and Osterville in 1922, and many agreed that a short series with only Cape League teams was the best thing. As a result, baseball on Cape Cod was about to enter a new era.

Chatham was one of four towns to have a team in the first year
(1923) of the brand new Cape Cod League.
Photo courtesy Tom Desmond.

· 2 ·

A Brand New Base Ball League

"Base ball excitement is running high in all the towns and a successful season is assured."
— Announcement in the July 9, 1923 issue of the *Hyannis Patriot*

Many historians argue that the Cape Cod Baseball League (CCBL) as it exists today was formed in 1923, when William J. Lovell of Hyannis, Harry Albro of Falmouth, J. Hubert Shepard of Chatham and Art Ayer of Osterville joined to form the first organized union. Disputing the Cape League's claims of an 1885 inception, they base their claims on the July 9, 1923 *Hyannis Patriot* article that was headlined "Cape Cod Baseball League." The story also said "A brand new base ball league was launched June 27th when representatives from Falmouth, Hyannis, Osterville and Chatham met and arranged a schedule of games for July and August. The teams meet each other four times, twice in each town, making twelve games to be played . . . The opening game was in Hyannis July 7th with Osterville for the opposing team."

The same announcement ran in the *Falmouth Enterprise,* another major Cape newspaper. It is believed that this account was the first time that the phrase "Cape Cod Baseball League" appeared in any publication.

The league soon attracted a collection of locals, ex-minor

leaguers, high schoolers, collegians, and paid semipros from throughout the Cape. They were mostly looking to pick up some extra money over the summer months playing baseball for their town team.

William Lovell was named league president, while Shepard acted as vice-president. Albro was the secretary, and Ayer served as the treasurer. However, it was Lovell who was the real driving force behind the league. A Barnstable selectman, he was a rabid baseball fan and an excellent organizer. One of the more popular men in Barnstable at the time, a 1960 article in the *Patriot* called him "the Branch Rickey of the Cape League."

In the 1920s, Lovell owned a clothing store on Main Street, and loved to promote himself, his store, and baseball (although not always in that order) with a bluster that was rare, even in the roaring '20s. He was always featuring outlandish sales on his merchandise, once giving away a dollar bill to each customer who walked into his store and bought something. He once headlined a newspaper advertisement for one of his stores with the words: "I have a vital message for you. 'I'M THE MAN.'" The words were splashed across the top of the page in large, boldfaced type.

While Lovell was a flamboyant self-promoter, Ayer was much more reserved. He was a dedicated baseball man, and had been instrumental in helping Somerville High build some of the best schoolboy teams in the country in the early 20th century. Nicknamed "Dutch," he had his Osterville teams play on West Bay Field, built over an abandoned cranberry bog.

Ayer developed a scrupulous reputation for fairness. In 1929, working as a league umpire, he ended up making a call against his hometown Osterville team. After a well-hit ball had been lost in a clump of bushes beyond the playing field, he ruled that the Osterville hitter should receive a double, and not a home run. Predictably, he received grief from the Osterville players, as well as Osterville manager Eddie McGrath, who lost the game because of the call. But the *Falmouth Enterprise* said that Ayer stuck to his call, reporting that despite the situation that "nearly resulted in a riot," he "refused to be phased (*sic*) by threats of violence and reverse his decision."

Cape Cod Baseball League

A brand new base ball league was launched June 27th when representatives from Falmouth, Hyannis, Osterville and Chatham met and arranged a schedule of games for July and August.

The teams meet each other four times, twice in each town, making twelve games to be played. The opening game was in Hyannis July 7th with Osterville for the opposing team.

Base ball excitement is running high in all the towns and a successful season is assured. William Lovell of Hyannis is President, J. H. Shepard of Chatham is Vice President, Mr. Albro of Falmouth, Secretary and Mr. Ayer of Osterville, Treasurer of the new organization.

Above: The first use of the phrase "Cape Cod Baseball League" to be found in the media. This announcement, published in the *Hyannis Patriot* on July 9, 1923, was also published in the *Falmouth Enterprise*.
Below: Earlier that summer, an announcement was made in the *Hyannis Patriot* heralding the imminent arrival of the Hyannis team. Reproduction courtesy of the *Barnstable Patriot*.

HYANNIS BASEBALL

Hyannis is to be represented this summer with a first class ball team, composed of college and preparatory school players. The team will be under the direction of Walter Snell, head coach of athletics, Brown University. The season is to open on July 4th. Morning and afternoon games with the Okos of Brockton.

Ayer apparently wasn't afraid to take part in a Cape League contest. In the late stages of the 1925 season, the *Falmouth Enterprise* noted that in the 11th inning of a contest between Falmouth and Hyannis, the former Somerville High baseball coach pinch-ran for Falmouth and scored the game-winner in a 1–0 nailbiter.

"The league was founded to add something for the summer people," Hal Goodenough told the *Cape Cod Times* in 1976. Goodenough played for Chatham in 1924, and went on to become the promotional director of the Milwaukee Braves and New York Mets. "The fans followed us everywhere. There was a real feeling of *esprit de corps* between the fans and the teams. We were often invited over to people's houses. They were just very, very friendly and generous. I look back on it as the time of my life playing on the Cape."

"It was a smattering of high schoolers, recent high school graduates, college youngsters coming home, who were summering in the area, former major and minor league players and old-timers," said Jack Aylmer, who played for Barnstable in the early days of the league. "I can remember some ballplayers in their 30s and 40s playing in the Cape League."

But in stark contrast to the major leagues, who were attracting mostly working-class country boys at this time, the Cape League featured well-mannered, polite young men, many of them from local colleges. The advertisement that ran in the *Barnstable Patriot* promoting the 1923 Hyannis team said that "Hyannis is to be represented this summer with a first class ball team, composed of college and preparatory school players."

A check of the 1925 Osterville roster that went on to win the league title indicates many locals and high school coaches. But players from Boston College, Springfield College, Brown University and Dartmouth dominated the roster. It may have been a blue collar sport throughout the rest of the country, but it was quickly becoming the sport of bluebloods on Cape Cod.

"In my time, the few big leaguers that I knew were on the hard-drinking side," said Tod Owen, who played for one of several Falmouth club teams in the early 20th century. "I went to New

Bedford and played a couple of games, and there were some pretty tough guys on that team. Not like the Cape."

Games were attended by people from all walks of life, with many of the more affluent patrons watching from the parked cars along the hillsides. And the early league drew many fans. For a game involving Osterville and Barnstable, there could be up to 1,000 people at Hallett's Field in Barnstable, watching the two best teams of the early days do battle.

CAPE BASEBALL SNAPSHOTS
The 1923 Season: Starting on the Right Foot

As noted earlier, most town histories and newspaper reports indicate that the Cape Cod Baseball League (CCBL) was formed in 1923, when William J. Lovell of Hyannis, Harry Albro of Falmouth, J. Hubert Shepard of Chatham and Art Ayer of Osterville joined to form the first organized union.

The Cape Cod League, as it was called then, began play on the first week of July, 1923. It was a week when Boston was paralyzed by a telephone operators strike. Filene's Department Store was offering men's "high-grade" shirts for $1.35, flannel coats for $2.55 and silk dresses for $7.50. Preparations were being made throughout Massachusetts for Independence Day celebrations, and President Harding's wife said that he would definitely be a candidate for re-election.

In sports, the big fight between Jack Dempsey and Tom Gibbons taking place in Shelby, Montana was on everyone's mind. Over 9,000 Boston fight fans crowded onto Boston's "Newspaper Row" to hear updates of the 15-round donnybrook, which was won by Dempsey.

But despite the fortunes of the seventh place Braves and the last place Red Sox, baseball was what gripped eastern Massachusetts on a daily basis throughout the month. Box scores and game stories from not only the two professional baseball teams in Boston, but also news about high school and semiprofessional teams filled the sports pages. And in the first week of July, 1923, the big news was a rumored sale of the last place Red Sox to a syndicate from

Columbus, Ohio, led by Bob Quinn. The rumor was roundly denied by Red Sox owner Harry Frazee. On July 7th, in the midst of the news about the rumored sale, came a 27-3 Red Sox loss at the hands of the Indians. The loss remains to this day the worst defeat that the storied franchise has ever endured. It is not known if the crushing loss affected the chances of the sale, but the Red Sox remained Frazee's property until 1933, when he sold the club — and Fenway Park — to Tom Yawkey.

If the newspapers were any measure, the inauguration of the CCBL was greeted on the Cape with a collective yawn. There were occasional missives in the weekly *Hyannis Patriot* and *Falmouth Enterprise,* but nothing more. At this time, the *Patriot* was more of a social newsletter than a newspaper. A typical front page would feature real-estate transactions, as well as notices about where people were spending their summer.

That's not to say that local papers didn't have occasionally insightful coverage of the action. A July 16th item in the *Patriot* under the Osterville town notes read: "Osterville ball team played with the Sandwich team Thursday. The game was a tie. Nearly 300 people went from Osterville to see the game."

According to most contemporary accounts, the league drew fairly well. Most crowds averaged anywhere between 100 and 400 fans. Games were played in various locations throughout the four towns.

The game was not limited to Falmouth, Hyannis, Chatham, and Osterville. Teams were forming throughout the Cape, regardless of their association with what was now the top circuit. In the August 6th issue of the *Patriot,* under the heading of "Legal Notices," appeared the following ad: "WANTED — Baseball team to play every Saturday during season with Wellfleet team at Wellfleet; also 'double-header' morning and afternoon, Labor Day, 1923." In addition, the *Patriot* reported on games from such far-flung places as Wareham. In one battle between Sandwich and Wareham, the *Patriot* indicated that Sandwich picked up the 5-4 win in a "finely played game" that featured a young man named Morrow "pitching his very best, and having good support in the outfield."

It is not known if the team from Wellfleet actually found an opponent for their Labor Day doubleheader, or how young Morrow did the rest of the season, but these are just two examples of how the game was catching on throughout the area. A July 23rd note in the *Patriot* under the Sandwich section said the following: "What would baseball players do without the support of the 'fans?' What care they, if a lady hustled the length of Main street (*sic*) in her kitchen apron, so anxious she was to get to the ball field and 'root.'"

As the season continued, baseball began to receive more and more coverage in the *Patriot*, with Chatham reporting scores to go along with the occasional notes from other locales. As the season wore on, standings as well as schedules were published. As a result, attendance often increased.

But it was Falmouth that seemed to be the class of the league in that first year, racing to an early lead and holding on through the summer. And as Cape Codders mourned the death of President Warren Harding (and held their breath as Massachusetts native Calvin Coolidge took over the reins of government), they prepared for the Barnstable Fair, to be held on August 28th through the 30th.

For Cape baseball fans, this year would be special. It would be the first time that strictly Cape teams would be playing at the Fair, and for what many believed would be the first-ever championship of the Cape Cod Baseball League.

Falmouth was the heavy favorite, having coasted to victory over Hyannis, Osterville, and Chatham. On August 20th, the *Patriot* reported that the playoff schedule had been set. Falmouth was to meet Hyannis on Tuesday, August 28th, while Chatham and Osterville were set to do battle the following afternoon. The winners would advance to the finals on Thursday, August 30th, the last day of the Fair.

With upset being the word of the day, Hyannis topped Falmouth by a 14–13 count. Despite the bad weather on Wednesday, Osterville beat Chatham by a 4–3 score. On Thursday, with over 3,000 people at the Fair, Hyannis captured the title with a 1–0 victory over Osterville. The *Patriot* would later say that "the baseball features were snappy and well-contested."

1926 SCHEDULE CAPE COD BASE BALL LEAGUE

	At CHATHAM	At FALMOUTH	At HYANNIS	At OSTERVILLE
CHATHAM		Wed. July 7 Sat. July 17 Fri. July 30 Sat. Aug. 7 Thurs. Aug. 12 Sat. Aug. 28 Mon. Sept. 6 A.M. (BARNSTABLE)	Mon. July 5 Fri. July 9 Sat. July 24 Wed. July 28 Tues. Aug. 3 Wed. Aug. 11 Sat. Aug. 21	Sat. July 3 Mon. July 19 Thurs. July 29 Sat. Aug. 14 Tues. Aug. 17 Wed. Aug. 25 Sat. Sept. 4
FALMOUTH	Fri. July 2 Tues. July 13 Fri. July 23 Tues. July 27 Fri. Aug. 20 Tues. Aug. 24 Wed. Sept. 1 (Fair)		Sat. July 3 Thurs. July 15 Thurs. July 22 Thurs. Aug. 5 Fri. Aug. 13 Tues. Aug. 17 Fri. Aug. 27	Mon. July 5 *A.M. Fri. July 9 Sat. July 31 Tues. Aug. 3 Fri. Aug. 6 Tues. Aug. 10 Mon. Aug. 30
HYANNIS	Mon. July 5 Tues. July 20 Sat. July 31 Fri. Aug. 6 Tues. Aug 10 Wed. Aug. 18 Mon. Aug. 23	Sat. July 10 Wed. July 14 Wed. July 21 Wed. Aug. 4 Sat. Aug. 14 Wed. Aug. 25 Sat. Sept. 4		Thurs. July 1 Mon. July 12 Sat. July 17 Fri. July 23 Fri. Aug. 20 Sat. Aug. 28 Tues. Aug. 31 (FAIR)
OSTERVILLE	Sat. July 10 Thurs. July 15 Wed. July 21 Wed. Aug. 4 Fri. Aug. 13 Thurs. Aug. 19 Fri. Aug. 27	Mon. July 5 *P.M. Sat. July 24 Wed. July 28 Wed. Aug. 11 Wed. Aug. 18 Sat. Aug. 21 Thurs. Aug. 26	Wed. July 7 Fri. July 16 Tues. July 27 Fri. July 30 Sat. Aug. 7 Tues. Aug. 24 Mon. Sept. 6 *P.M. (BARNSTABLE)	

By 1926, the Cape League had become important enough to have the complete schedule published in most area papers. By this time, all teams were playing upwards of 40 games a year, not including exhibition and playoff contests. Reproduction courtesy of the *Barnstable Patriot*.

· 3 ·

The Roaring ´20s

"Cape Cod is fortunate in having a national pastime played
in a recognized and organized league. It's a great game."
— *Hyannis Patriot* article, August 20, 1936

Before the 1924 season, the Barnstable town meeting appropriated
money for the two Barnstable teams. The *Patriot* supported the
funding because baseball "helped our hotel keepers and merchants," and some of the visitors who were attracted by the league
"have expressed a wish to buy land and build."

The league was just one of several attractions that the Cape
hoped would lure tourists throughout the 1920s. With the surge
of tourist dollars that had recently poured into the state of Florida,
Cape Cod entrepreneurs expressed a sincere desire to turn the Cape
into the same sort of vacation outpost, despite the wish of many
native Cape Codders that the tourists would leave them alone. In
the fight for tourists, the Cape first made its presence felt on the
national level in the late ´20s. The *Cape Cod Magazine* predicted
that "A few professional developers such as have been successful
elsewhere, could transform Cape Cod into a second Florida within
two or three years time."

And transform it they did. Realtors and developers swarmed
the area, changing the sleepy seaside peninsula into a tourist mecca

virtually overnight. According to a report in August, 1926, two men, working in shifts, during a 13-hour period had counted 16,258 cars passing the intersection of Barnstable Road, Main Street, and Ocean Street in Hyannis. These were the sort of statistics that helped to feed the frenzy among Cape businesses and helped to create the mystique of the Cape as a vacation hotspot that continues to this day.

But despite the financial boom that the rest of the Cape was enjoying in the 1920s, there wasn't any real financial stability in the early years of the league. In addition to the original four, teams from Barnstable Village, along with clubs from Bourne, Harwich, Orleans, and Wareham dropped in and out of the league through-out the 1920s. In addition, umpiring soon became a concern. The *Barnstable Patriot* said at the end of the 1926 season that "many of the games this summer were obviously marred by the kind of um-piring received . . . Some go as far as saying that umpiring ruined baseball on Cape Cod." During that year, many umpires simply didn't show up at the game. One writer recalled a game between Chatham and Falmouth where no umpires showed up, so the writer himself called the balls and strikes.

But while teams began with a limited schedule in the early days of the league, that soon changed. As early as the 1926 season, teams were playing more than 40 games a year, not including exhibitions and possible playoff contests. And the clubs did not limit them-selves to interleague play. The 1933 season saw many of the clubs face the Norfolk Prison Colony Outfit, managed by Hyannis na-tive Herbert O. Bacon, Jr. Despite some initial trepidation on the part of many of the league's executive committee, the exhibitions went off without a hitch. Hyannis and Falmouth both faced teams from the Cuban Giants and the House of David during the 1927 campaign. Despite a valiant effort from Hyannis, the "long-haired visitors" (as the *Patriot* called the House of David squad) won by a 2–1 count.

When league officials and the leaders of the Barnstable County Fair couldn't reach agreement on how much the league would be paid for staging their championships on the grounds, the way was paved for what many believe was the first baseball contest to include black players on Cape Cod. In fact, it was this decision that solidified the creation of a Cape-only league. According to a report in the August 29, 1925 issue of the *Falmouth Enterprise,* fair officials had increased the price of admission to the annual festival, and they refused to grant the Cape teams more money for expenses. To get back at the fair officials, the teams scheduled "bargain" doubleheaders on each day of the fair, going head-to-head for the entertainment dollar. It is not clear who made out better, but the fair apparently didn't take the challenge sitting down. On the same page that the report ran, a large advertisement for the Barnstable Fair trumpeted: "Baseball at the Fair! Philadelphia Giants vs. East Boston All-Stars. All three days. Sept. 1–2–3 1925." The Philadelphia Colored Giants played in New England many times throughout the 1920s and 1930s. In the summer of 1925, they had a 58–10 mark, and were considered by many to be the best semipro club in the Northeast.

In 1929, Falmouth faced the Boston Braves, but lost by an 8–7 count in an early-season exhibition. At the time, the *Brockton Enterprise* noted that "The caliber of ball in the league is being recognized by all the Boston experts as about as good as can be found outside the big show."

And in 1934, a team from the *U.S.S. Hopkins* played Cape League teams from Barnstable, Falmouth, and Harwich, as well as an exhibition in Provincetown. Halfway through the 1996 season, the all-female Colorado Silver Bullets faced a squad of Cape Leaguers during the league's All-Star break. Despite the first outside-the-park home run in Bullets history coming off the bat of Kim Braatz, the Cape Leaguers emerged victorious by a 4–1 count.

The '20s were replete with interesting moments. The 1926 season ended with co-champions, Hyannis and Osterville. After a frantic pennant race that saw the two teams tied at the end of the season, both teams decided to face each other in a one-game playoff.

Osterville was ready with Harry Vernon, a "mystery pitcher" who had tremendous success whenever he faced his old team in Hyannis. On the other side, Hyannis readied Joel Sherman, an excellent pitcher in his own right who had beaten Falmouth by a

"Deacon" Danny MacFayden is considered to be the finest
baseball player ever born on Cape Cod. Born in North Truro,
MacFayden went on to a long professional career with the
Red Sox and Yankees. Photo courtesy of Al Irish.

5–1 count the previous Saturday, allowing Hyannis to pull into a first place tie with Osterville.

But a late summer downpour (the *Barnstable Patriot* said "Old Joe Pluto let loose the heavens") forced a postponement. When Hyannis manager Freddie Moncewicz, a 22-year-old who also doubled as a shortstop and would later go on to play with the Red Sox, conferred with the Osterville manager the next day, they found it impossible to pick a future date. The rosters of both teams would be decimated by losses, most players being called back to campus by their college football coaches or to their jobs by their bosses. The season ended with Hyannis and Osterville agreeing to share the title of champion. In the same spirit of sharing, the towns of Harwich and Chatham shared a franchise in 1927. Chatham received its own franchise the next year, and Harwich received its own franchise three years later.

Osterville's appearance in the championship game was no fluke, as the village was a baseball hotbed throughout the '20s and '30s. One of the seven villages of Barnstable, Osterville fielded competitive clubs for many years. Players like "Deacon" Danny MacFayden and Shanty Hogan would go on to long careers at the major league level, but both of them started in Osterville.

MacFayden could have been the most famous Cape native to make it to the major leagues. Born in North Truro on June 10, 1905, he attended Somerville High. After graduation, he soon returned to the Cape in the early '20s like many other young ballplayers, hoping to use the Cape League as a steppingstone to the majors. He played for both Falmouth and Osterville, helping the latter win the 1924 league title with a 9–2 mark as a pitcher and a .282 mark at the plate when playing the outfield.

While on the Cape, his performances were usually nothing short of impressive. But perhaps his most memorable achievement came while he was pitching for Falmouth in 1925. Against Hyannis, he held a no-hitter into the bottom of the ninth inning. But with two outs, it was broken up by a routine single to right field.

MacFayden reached the majors two years later, pitching for the Boston Red Sox. He had a six-year career with the Sox, posting a 16–12 mark in 1931. However, like most Boston talent of the day, he was sold to the Yankees near the beginning of the 1932 season. While with the Yankees, he played alongside legends such as Ruth and Gehrig, helping New York win the 1932 World Series. After a couple of seasons in New York, he returned home to Boston — after a short stay with the Cincinnati Reds — albeit this time in the National League. He pitched for the Braves from 1936 through 1939, posting a career-high 17 wins in his first season with the Braves. After recording seasons of 14, 14, and eight wins with the Braves, he rounded out his major league career with stops in Pittsburgh, Washington, and again with the Braves before calling it quits at the age of 37. He died in 1972 in Brunswick, Maine.

But Osterville also had its share of offbeat characters, one of them being Frank Bearse. Nicknamed "Seven-Inning Spitball," he was one of the true characters of the league in the '20s and '30s, but that didn't mean he couldn't pitch. The *Falmouth Enterprise* said in a July 26, 1928 story: "Bearse of Osterville has more 'stuff' than any pitcher in the league and when he can control it, it is unbeatable. He is a real Cape Codder too."

One of the toughest pitchers in the league at the time, Bearse was usually untouchable until the seventh inning, when he would tire and start to walk a few batters, at which point the opposing fans would start razzing him mercilessly.

Bearse would then proceed to stomp around the mound, clearly upset and rattled. Then, he would reach into his back pocket for a piece of bark from a slippery elm tree. After tearing off a piece of the bark and placing it in his mouth, he would spit on the baseball. Fans, umpires, and opposing players would complain, but Bearse would open his mouth and there wouldn't be a trace of the slippery elm to be seen.

He would laugh, and stomp around the mound, waving his arms. While many of his opponents were complaining to the umpires, the umpires would laugh. Many remember Danny Silva, who would go on to become commissioner of the league, yelling at Bearse: "Come on Frankie, let's get down to business. It's getting late."

With the opposing batters usually psyched out by this point, and standing way off the plate, he would proceed to work his way out of the jam with his exaggerated, windmill delivery and with the suspected help of the bark of the slippery elm.

Another notable Osterville player of the era who might have fallen into the same category was Shanty Hogan. Hogan was one player who took advantage of the fans' custom of bringing home-baked treats to their favorite players. Whether it was cake, cookies or brownies, many can remember players running to the plate with their bat in one hand and a piece of food in the other.

After his time with Osterville, the 6-foot, 250-pound Hogan would go on to a 13-year career with the Boston Braves, New York Giants, and Washington Senators. During his career, he would play for the great John McGraw and catch such legendary pitchers as Carl Hubbell. But he was also one of the largest men to play the game during his time in the majors in the '20s and '30s. He was in the company of players such as Gob Buckeye (6', 260 pounds) and Jumbo Brown (6'4", 295 pounds).

Even though Hogan was a defensive standout (he led the league twice in fielding percentage and once in putouts), solid at the plate (a .295 career batting average), and a smart man on the base paths (he finished with 12 triples and six steals in his major league career), he would be out of the game at the age of 31, a victim of his poor eating habits. The *Barnstable Patriot* would later call it a "shame . . . that such a fine man would literally eat his way out of the game."

The 1928 season was an extraordinary one at the major league level. Babe Ruth and the powerful New York Yankees had managed to restore the nation's confidence in a game that had been shaken by the 1919 Black Sox scandal. Ruth hit 54 home runs as the Yankees faced Rogers Hornsby (who hit .387 that season for the Cardinals) and St. Louis in the World Series. But the mighty Yankee machine was too much for the Cardinals, crushing them 4–0 in the Fall Classic.

And it was the first year that several former Cape Leaguers were actually seen at the major league level. Former Osterville pitcher and North Truro native "Deacon" Danny MacFayden went 9–15, throwing 195 innings and posting a 4.75 ERA for the Red

Sox. Disputed Cape Leaguer Mickey Cochrane would be the starting catcher for a Philadelphia Athletics team that would win 98 games, but finish 2 1/2 games behind the legendary Yankees of Ruth and Gehrig. Another player with a disputed time in the Cape League was Pie Traynor, who hit .337 while handling the hot corner that season for the Pirates.

But maybe the most heartwarming story of a player to make it to the majors out of the Cape League that year was that of former Hyannis manager and shortstop Freddie Moncewicz. He was a teammate of MacFayden, and realized every New England kid's dream of playing in Fenway Park.

Another major boost for the Cape League came later that same year, when the Boston Twilight League took the unprecedented action of banning from their circuit any players who played in the Cape League. The Twilight League was long considered a staple of semipro baseball throughout New England, and the move they made was important. The Twilight League had often considered themselves better than the Cape League. With the mere mention of them in the same breath, the Cape Leaguers knew that they had risen to the same level as the popular, more established Twilighters. The Cape League's response followed soon after, and was published in the *Patriot*:

> "... the Cape Cod League goes merrily along about its business, produces good ball, attracts only high grade, gentlemanly ball players and satisfactorily entertains the nation's vacationing mayors, public officials and men of influence. Cape Cod calls and no punishment awaits those who answer."

At that time, Cape Cod baseball was divided into two leagues, the Upper Cape and the Lower Cape.

(NOTE: To understand the idea of the Upper and Lower Cape, one must look at Cape Cod geography with a unique form of native logic. While a layman might think that the Upper Cape would be the easternmost "upraised forearm" of the Cape, the reverse is true. The Upper Cape is its westernmost region, and the area in between is referred to as the mid-Cape.)

The two circuits operated separately, but they got along well. Each league had its own by-laws, administration, officers, and umpires. Teams from the two leagues did not play each other during the regular season, but there was an all-star game between the two, usually held in mid-August. Over Labor Day, winners of the two leagues met in a best-of-three series to determine the winner of the Cape Cod Baseball League. The relationship between the two leagues remained constant until the early '60s and is not unlike the current relationship enjoyed by the American and National Leagues.

All the teams were prosperous and attracted large crowds throughout the 1920s and 1930s. The supporters of the other leagues didn't hesitate to get in a gibe at the Cape Cod League. In a July 27, 1933 story in the *Hyannis Patriot*, a North Truro man let his feelings about the CCBL be known: "It is an unpleasant fact that there are so many unappreciative people in a community when a little recreation is offered for their entertainment. Some people will drive 10 miles or more to watch a ball game where the playing is no better and often much worse then (*sic*) what is shown on the home grounds."

The story went on to take a swipe at either the Cape League (or perhaps major league baseball) when it said: "If some people think that the only interesting games are where there is a howling mob of several thousand, then they have another guess coming."

It was also during this time that the league began gaining popularity among several talented semiprofessional and collegiate ballplayers around the country. It was viewed as an easy steppingstone for budding major leaguers. But even if they weren't on their way to the majors, many locals used the league as an opportunity to pick up some extra cash while playing for the local town team.

Despite the onset of the Depression, the league peaked in popularity in the mid-1930s. Hyannis even had a special "road team" as well as its own Industrial League club. A number of independent teams existed. The sport was so popular that a small town like Brewster supported two teams.

During the Depression, the sound of a firebell could cause a sudden mass exodus from a baseball game, as all able-bodied men

There were several teams and several leagues that popped up
prior to World War II. In 1935, the Chatham A.A. team won
the Barnstable County Twi-Title. Helping lead the team
was Merrill Doane (top right), a man who would
be instrumental in helping the Cape Cod
Baseball League make the transition into
the modern era in the 1960s.
In addition, Doane was the oldest player when the
Cape League held an Old-Timers Game to
celebrate its 100th anniversary in 1985.
Photo courtesy of Tom Desmond.

received $1.50 if they helped fight a fire. And the Depression soon began to play havoc with the league financially. Social commentators were divided in their opinions on how the money people did manage to have should be spent. "There seems to be an opinion among many that money that has been in the past devoted to baseball had better be used for the purchase of food and other necessities so that gate receipts are expected to be a good deal less," read a June 23, 1932 report in the *Hyannis Patriot*.

That year, in particular, was a difficult one, especially leading up to the first week of the season in July. As late as May 19, there were only two teams that had fully committed to the season. Falmouth and Harwich were ready to go, but Barnstable and Orleans were unsure because of a perceived lack of funds.

But the league pulled through, fielding a five-team circuit made up of Wareham, Harwich, Falmouth, Barnstable (which played its games at West Bay Field in Osterville because "there were no suitable grounds in Hyannis," said the *Patriot*) and Orleans.

Despite the league's growing popularity, it rarely extended beyond Orleans. On occasion, there were teams from North Truro and Eastham. Provincetown's only year in the league was 1933, when they finished dead last. In fact, they couldn't even finish out the year. Bourne filled in when Provincetown dropped out just after midseason. Bourne did its best under the circumstances, but posted an astoundingly poor 1–25 mark.

An important step was taken at the 1934 league meetings in Hyannis. Many thought that it would be a good idea to encourage teams from throughout southeastern Massachusetts to join the league, possibly increasing revenue and spreading popularity throughout the area. But the league officers decided to officially limit league members to Barnstable County only, closing the gates and making it a Cape-only league.

Town baseball on Nantucket and Martha's Vineyard continued to flourish, but their teams were never a part of the CCBL on a regular basis. However, in the 1920s, a four-team, recreational men's league provided the Islanders with baseball. Nantucket Historical Society records indicate that at one point these four teams combined to create an all-star club to face a frequent visitor to the

Cape, the Philadelphia Colored Giants. The Nantucketers were crushed, but it did not dampen their spirit for the game. Many islanders still hope for a team of their own, but most are happy watching the two or three games a year staged on the island by various Cape League clubs.

With the passing of the Depression, the Cape began to enjoy an unprecedented boom in the mid-1930s. The *Hyannis Patriot* hailed the opening of the Bourne Bridge on June 22, 1935 with the banner headline "Biggest Day in History of Cape." But as the league moved into the late '30s, the financial strains of times and conditions accompanying the onset of World War II began to catch up with the circuit. Barnstable folded in 1938, and Orleans stepped in. In 1939, Orleans folded and Barnstable re-entered the circuit. Midway through the 1939 season, Hyannis restaurateurs saved the league from collapse with a sizable donation. Teams once again started charging an admission of 25 cents a man (women and children were admitted free).

But the players, young or old, were simply happy to be doing a job that they loved.

"It was a time of no night games, indolent mornings of soaking up the sun at Bank Street Beach (in Harwich), bed and board provided free and a pay envelope handed out by the manager every Saturday morning from late June to around Labor Day," recalled former player Til Ferdenzi in a 1983 article in the *Cape Cod Times.*

Despite spending $860 on field improvements, including upgrading the playing area and adding bleachers, Barnstable finished the season with a surprisingly small deficit. In addition, several other teams reported that they either had a small surplus or had broken even. The league fathers sat down in mid-August to discuss the giddy prospect of expansion. It was agreed that Chatham would re-enter the league after a short absence. This served two purposes. First, it would spread the influence of the burgeoning circuit further throughout the Lower Cape. Second, it would allow all the teams to play every possible day. (At that time, the five-team format forced at least one team to sit idle every day.)

But baseball would not return to Barnstable for the 1938 season.

Despite an impressive run, they lost money, and the franchise had to bow out of the league. (They would return in 1939.) However, the lack of baseball in Barnstable that summer didn't mean that the townsfolk had lost their passion for the game. They enjoyed the Cape League over the 1938 campaign, and played an integral role that summer in a monumental event in league history.

Many histories indicate that the first night baseball game on the Cape took place in the summer of 1939 in Falmouth, but an August 18, 1938 story in the *Hyannis Patriot* reveals that Barnstable High played host to a night contest between Falmouth and the Philadelphia Colored Giants.

Falmouth triumphed by a 16–6 count, and Frank Benyon struck out 14 on the way to victory. But it was not the on-field activity that concerned league officials. They used an astonishing three dozen baseballs during the contest, with many of them simply not returned by fans who wanted a souvenir of the game. In addition, people were able to watch the game for free beyond the right field fence, subverting the admission charge. These factors made night baseball an expensive proposition for a league that was struggling to survive financially. The *Patriot* said: "There'll have to be better provisions for getting back the foul balls before the Cape League teams will be able to afford night ball."

In 1939, the tercentenary celebration was planned to mark the 300th anniversary of the Town of Barnstable. No simple event, it was scheduled to allow the citizens of the Cape to revel in their own fascination with the past. Included in these events was what many believe to be the first "old-timers" game on the Cape. The game was held in Barnstable between a select group of former Cape Leaguers and current Cape League All-Stars, with the old-timers emerging victorious.

After a relatively successful 1939 season that finished with five teams, towns began dropping out at an alarming rate. Falmouth, which had been a league stalwart since the CCL's inception in 1923, dropped out. At their annual town meeting in February, citizens rejected the team budget of $3,000, only appropriating $500 for a twilight league team.

Later that same month, league president Charles D. Holmes of Harwich confessed that things looked bleak for the 1940 campaign. "As much as I hate to admit it, I don't see how there can be a league this year," he admitted in the February 15, 1940 edition of the *Barnstable Patriot*. "It's too bad, especially because so many of the summer people enjoyed it, but the league looks finished for the year, anyway."

At this point, both Falmouth and Bourne had dropped out, citing financial constraints. Baseball fans in Barnstable held out hope that approval of their $3,000 request (which would be put to a vote at their town meeting in March) would help to save the rapidly shrinking league.

But pessimists realized that even if Barnstable came through, and Harwich stayed solvent, that would only leave the league with two teams. Even in previous years, with towns like Chatham, Wareham, and Provincetown adding a team, it probably wouldn't be enough to field a league for the 1940 season.

And then came the league's death knell. The March 7, 1940 edition of the *Barnstable Patriot* reported that "the requested $3,000 recreational appropriation formerly voted for baseball was turned down with hardly a word." However, like Falmouth, Barnstable allotted fewer funds for a twilight league team.

A last-minute meeting was held later that month, but it was to no avail. Baseball on Cape Cod was closing up shop, and wouldn't open again until after World War II.

Many would-be Cape Leaguers headed off to war, but it wasn't just the Cape League that lost many of their stars. Throughout the game of baseball, players like Ted Williams, Joe DiMaggio, and Bob Feller gave up the game for military duty. But unlike the majors, the Cape League found it almost impossible to survive without top drawer talent. Oddly, the September 7, 1939 issue of the *Barnstable Patriot* seemed to herald the silencing of baseball on Cape Cod:

"The Cape Cod League is one of the few projects carried on by towns on the Cape, cooperatively, to provide entertainment for summer folk. It will be a distinct loss to Cape Cod and to many communities if the league ceases to be."

But there was one last-ditch effort made to salvage something resembling Cape League action. In May of 1940, Dr. William H. Wallace of Roslindale and Cataumet came to the Falmouth Park Board with a proposal that would bring Boston Park League players to Falmouth Heights every Saturday and Sunday throughout the season. They promised pretty good baseball at no cost to the town, and the park board seemed ready to turn the field over to the Park Leaguers.

But the Falmouth twilight league didn't want to give up their ballpark on Sunday afternoon. When twilight league officials Louis Rabesa and John Pena went to the Park Board to protest, the board withdrew its invitation to Dr. Wallace, and that ended that.

CAPE BASEBALL SNAPSHOTS
1937 — A Pennant Race for the Ages

The year 1937 was a watershed one for the league. As America battled its way out of the Great Depression and closer to World War II, the national passion for the game of baseball reached a fever pitch. Players like Bob Feller, Joe DiMaggio, and Hank Greenberg had grabbed hold of the national consciousness, and refused to let go. Things were no different in eastern Massachusetts, as the Cape Cod League was now firmly established as one of the premier summer baseball leagues in the country, and a growing tourist attraction on the Cape.

Massachusetts Governor Charles F. Hurley got the 1937 season started in regal fashion, when he appeared with much fanfare on Saturday, July 3rd at the season opener between Orleans and Harwich. A veteran of many first ball ceremonies at Fenway, the Democrat eschewed the handshaking and baby-kissing that usually went along with an appearance of this nature. After arriving at the field, he quickly borrowed an umpire's cap, a glove from one of the players and dashed out to the mound to begin warming up for the inaugural toss.

"Batter Up" In Cape Cod League
Saturday at Hyannis and Orleans

Cape Cod Baseball league teams will open the 1937 season next Saturday afternoon at 3:30 p.m. in Hyannis and Orleans. Falmouth will cross bats at Barnstable high field with the Barnstable team, and Harwich invades Orleans for the lower Cape opener.

In Hyannis Manager Edward "Pete" Herman will again lead the Barnstable team. Games will be played at the high school field, at the foot of High School road, a few hundred yards south of Main street. Ample parking space for all automobiles is provided, and better seating accommodations than at old Hallett's field where the team played in other years. A big turnout is hoped for the first local game.

At Orleans the league opener will be a gala affair. Governor Charles F. Hurley will pitch out the first ball. The Orleans committee has prepared a big welcome for His Excellency, which includes a parade from Depot Square to the field. Just who will catch the first ball was in doubt this week, since league President William E. C. Perry of Bourne, a banker, can't get away to receive the Hurley toss.

As an indication of the better times which seem to be manifesting themselves around the nation, the Cape Cod League this year decided to restore the two-umpires-per-game system. For the past three seasons, but one ump per match could be afforded. This year Tom Whelan of English high, Lynn, was named umpire in chief. He chose Jack Walsh, Holbrook high coach and former Falmouth team manager; Danny Silva, former Osterville player, and Walter F. Pearce, who used to call them in the Nova Scotia league, to work the Cape.

Cape Cod league games, it was voted, will all begin at 3:30 p.m. this season save at Bourne, where the working class demands a 4 p.m. starting time except on Saturdays, Sundays and holidays. The schedule calls for a season of 120 games, not divided in mid-season with a winner of the first half announced, but played through to the end.

Rosters of the five Cape league teams were announced at the league directors meeting in Hyannis town building Monday night as follows:

BARNSTABLE

Edward "Pete" Herman, coach at Kents Hill prep, in Maine, will again be skipper for the Barnstable team. His roster of players includes John "Muggsy" Kelley of Boston College, Norman Mirrell of John Carroll, and John Maloney of Kents Hill, as pitchers, with Pete himself taking an occasional turn. Stanley Bergeron of Bates at first; Francis "Cowboy" Crawley of Villanova, at second; Paul Sharkey of B. C. at shortstop; and Roy Williams of English high, Boston, at 3rd. For outfield Herman will have: John Spirada of St. Anselms. Guy Vitale of Colgate, and Tim Ready of B. C. as utility. George Colbert of B. C. will catch. Robert "Bob" Cash of Hyannis and B. C. will pitch, if he doesn't respond to the Nova Scotian league lure.

FALMOUTH

William J. "Bill" Boehner Jr., former B.C. star, who played in the Cape league first for Falmouth, then handled Harwich in 1936, returns to Falmouth this year to fill the boots of veteran Jack Walsh, Falmouth manager for six years. Boehner has signed up the following players:

William Ryan, Holy Cross, as catcher; Roy Bruninghau of Holy

Continued on Page 3

The *Hyannis Patriot* heralds the opening of the 1937. One of the most dramatic seasons in Cape League history, it would showcase an epic battle between Barnstable, Falmouth, Orleans, Bourne and Harwich for the league title that wouldn't be decided until the final day of the season. Reproduction courtesy of the *Barnstable Patriot*.

A steady rain began to fall and the Governor was asked if he wanted to seek shelter. Hurley would have none of it. The ballplayers looked at each other anxiously, as the game was set to begin. However, Hurley continued warming up in the rain without a care.

"It's not the first time the Governor was all wet on Cape Cod," league officer and longtime Republican Harry Albro muttered quietly as both teams waited for the Governor to finish warming up so the game could begin.

Eventually the Governor was ready. It was reported that his pitch was a "low one," but the batter swung and missed good-naturedly. Almost immediately, the Governor and his party were whisked back to Boston.

Harwich beat Orleans in the season opener, but the real action was in Bourne. It was here that Barnstable and Bourne would play the first of several tight ballgames over the course of the season.

Bourne led 10–7 entering the top of the ninth, and it looked as though the defending champions would have their first win of the season at the expense of the team that had been picked by many to take the 1937 title. But Barnstable scored three in the top of the ninth, and added four in the tenth to surprise the Canalmen by a 14–10 count. The game featured superb relief work from Norman Merrill (nicknamed "the Man from Maine" by the *Hyannis Patriot*), out of John Carroll College in Maine. It would not be the last time that Bourne heard from Merrill.

During the season, four of the five teams staged epic battles for first place. Harwich, Falmouth, and Bourne joined Barnstable in a season-long race, and it was clear from the start that the race wouldn't be decided until the last day of the season at the Barnstable Fair Grounds.

Home to Cape Cod's largest year-round population, Barnstable featured some of the best baseball on the Cape in the early days of the league. Under the legendary manager Pete Herman, the team had been near or at the top of the league since the early '20s. They played at Hallett's Field, on Main Street. In addition to functioning as the town ball field and the site of several civic and athletic activities, it also served as an arbitrary boundary separating the summer and year-round business districts in Hyannis.

Throughout the league, it was regarded as one of the nicer fields despite a public road that ran through deep left centerfield. However, as early as 1932, the Barnstable team began talking about moving from the cozy confines at Hallett's Field, explaining that there was a need for larger quarters. They were no doubt mindful of the danger that threatened the left and center fielders when they had to cross the road to field their positions. As a result, many of the games that were home games for the Barnstable or Hyannis teams were played at West Bay Field in Osterville, an area surrounded by a cranberry bog, because as the *Hyannis Patriot* had said as early as 1932 that there were "no suitable grounds in Hyannis." Hallett's Field was eventually bulldozed in 1954.

At one time, Barnstable had on its roster the greater part of the "Million Dollar Infield of College Baseball" — Hank O'Day at third, Fred Moncewicz and/or Paddy Creedon at second, and Pete Herman at first.

After they played in the Cape League, most of the quartet went on to extremely successful careers. Moncewicz, after playing briefly with the Red Sox, became the State of Massachusetts Comptroller, Creedon became the Director of Physical Education for the State Department, and Herman developed into one of the best-liked and most successful schoolboy coaches in America at Kent's Hill Preparatory School in Maine.

Another Barnstable player of note during the glory days was Eddie Gallagher, a huge, 6'4", 225-pound man who was a superb pitcher. Gallagher later signed with the Red Sox, and was working as their batting practice pitcher when he was hit in the leg by a line drive. He was hospitalized, and later forced to undergo an operation. As a result of this accident, the Red Sox placed a net in front of their batting practice pitcher, a practice that continues to this day.

In the 1930s, the Barnstable pitching staff wasn't always good, but the fearsome lineup of hitters kept opposing pitching staffs in trouble. When people imitate the Cape by forming their arm into an uppercut, it is Barnstable that is the muscle. And that's exactly what Barnstable was at the plate over the course of the 1930s, and 1937 in particular.

Barnstable's version of Murderer's Row featured George Colbert, a catcher from Boston College, who frequently led the league in home runs, and led all of college baseball during his sophomore season with a .428 batting average; Ken Strong, a first baseman and legendary slugger from New York University; Vernon Bearse, a pitcher who was so fearsome with the bat that he frequently lofted home runs over Weber's Clock Shop on North Street, estimated to be close to 450 feet from home plate. Other star players such as Arthur Staff, who went on to coach some of the best players in Massachusetts history while he was head coach at Brockton High; Hugh McNulty, one of the leading college baseball players in the '30s out of Boston College, and Roland "Lefty" Barker, one of the best pitchers/outfielders of the era, who played for Dartmouth College.

But it was George Colbert who was remembered down through the years as the likeable, happy-go-lucky player who kept everyone loose. Frequent opponent Bill Carpenter of Osterville recalled the antics of his longtime friend on the occasion of Colbert's death in a *Cape Cod Times* appreciation:

> "He believed in entertaining the fans," Carpenter said. "He refused to take the game seriously and was always a big favorite with the people. I remember the time when he was catching a pitcher who wasn't very fast. He caught him bare-handed for an inning. The fans loved it."

Barnstable fans played a large role in the diamond goings-on. A group of diehard female fans warned the team they would boycott the remaining games if Colbert was traded near the end of the 1937 season for more pitching. Two other women claimed credit for a Barnstable victory when they donated their headbands and shoestrings to the pitching staff to use as good luck charms. The fans supported their team with chants of "Into the Silverleaves!

Into the Silverleaves!" for the trees beyond the outfield or "Over Weber's! Over Weber's!" in reference to Weber's Clock Shop on North Street, made famous with baseball fans because of several of Vernon Bearse's monumental clouts.

In addition, many of the Barnstable players endeared themselves to fans with their antics. Several players, including Norman Merrill, would regularly infuriate the opposition with frequent laughing, razzing, and high-pitched whistling. Merrill, who coached third base for much of the season, frequently came under attack from other teams as he taunted them from his coach's box. The players were also in demand for personal appearances. The entire team appeared at the Barnstable Carnival in late August in a game of "donkey baseball," playing against a team of high school all-stars. The game was a wild hit, and raised money for the Barnstable Athletic Association.

But it was manager Pete Herman who was the real hero. Perhaps the first well-known manager in the Cape League, Herman managed the wildly successful Barnstable clubs which featured some of the most powerful lineups of the era and would come to be known as "Herman's Hitters." He was so beloved by his players that after Barnstable clinched the 1934 title, the players surrounded him and all took turns congratulating him instead of celebrating amongst themselves.

A September 6, 1934 story in the *Hyannis Patriot* recalls Herman's rapport with players and fans: "Pete had the interest of the team and town at heart every minute since the first ball was thrown out at Osterville and the flag was raised at Hallett's field (*sic*). The fellows are loud in their praise of his knowledge of the game and of his personal interest in them. No manager has worked more faithfully in taking care of the fields, looking after his players, hustling to win and trying to give the fans a championship club."

The Barnstable fans read about their heroes in the largest newspaper on the Cape, the *Hyannis Patriot*. The *Patriot* provided comprehensive coverage of all league action with front-page wrapups of the week's action, complete with standings and a baseball notebook called "Batteries for Barnstable: Base Hits and Breezy Bits."

But the big news during the month of July, 1937 was Alton Sherman and his record-setting flight in a beechcraft plane — from New York to Hyannis — in just under an hour. July was also welcomed with a heat wave that gripped the Cape during most of the summer, with the temperature on Main Street in Hyannis frequently topping out over 100 degrees. The hot weather proved to be just the tonic for the Barnstable offense. A mid-July contest between Barnstable and Falmouth saw 25 runs come across the plate, including nine home runs. In that contest, Barnstable pulled out an improbable 13–12 win in 12 innings.

But the Bourne team wasn't ready to roll over. They scratched and clawed their way back. With Barnstable going into a prolonged slump as the season wore on, the teams grew closer and closer. And on September 2, Bourne led Barnstable by five percentage points with less than a week to play.

Things were growing worrisome for the Barnstable team. An easygoing bunch suddenly became tense and irritable, losing three in a row as the season dwindled down to a few remaining games. Herman confessed to losing some weight and hair over his predicament, and privately worried about losing his job if he allowed Bourne to overtake them. The *Patriot* reported that "[the fans] do not know how their nervous systems can carry them through until Labor Day." As the race grew tighter and the days clicked off the calendar, fans and media alike pointed to the last day of the season, when a contest between Bourne and Barnstable could well decide the season.

On Monday, September 6th, the final day of the regular season, and as the 1937 season entered the final day, the standings were as follows:

TEAM	W	L
Barnstable	28	17
Bourne	26	17
Harwich	25	19
Falmouth	23	22
Orleans	9	36

Bourne was scheduled to face Barnstable and then Orleans in a doubleheader. If Bourne could win both games, they could complete their improbable comeback and force a playoff game for the title.

Despite a sunny sky and a stiff breeze, the Barnstable field was in less than stellar condition. A nasty storm had lashed the Cape the night before, and forced the players to contend with what the *Patriot* called "football weather." Barnstable groundskeeper Jim Anderson (who also worked as a "ticket-taker and information-giver," according to the *Patriot*) began his chores at eight o'clock that morning, using sand and sawdust to get the field ready for the 10:30 A.M. start.

Despite his team's slump, Herman felt confident. He had Norman Merrill on the mound, and Merrill had been death on the league all year, posting a 12–3 mark entering the contest, including a 3–0 mark for the season against Bourne. When he wasn't pitching, he was also one of the league's leading hitters, finishing with a .394 average, and adding three home runs for good measure.

Bourne wasn't as sure. Manager Larry Donovan knew he had a good club, but the recent string of back-to-back games caused by bad weather had put a terrific strain on his pitching staff. Over the last week, he had been pulling a smoke-and-mirrors act, winning with guile instead of talent, sheer will and determination rather than ability.

The game got under way before 500 fans, and through the first three innings neither team was able to score. But in the bottom of the fourth, Barnstable erupted for three runs to take the lead. Meanwhile, Merrill had not allowed Bourne to make a hit. Barnstable added single runs in the fifth and seventh, as Merrill continued to bewitch the bewildered Bourne ballplayers. Despite two runners who reached base due to error, he continued his no-hit performance into the ninth.

Despite an increasing wind, Merrill continued to work his magic. Keeping in mind that they only needed one win to take the crown, Merrill set down the Bourne team in order in the ninth inning to finish off his no-hitter. The Barnstable players were the league champions, and Norman Merrill had solidified his position as one of the best clutch performers in Cape League history.

Barnstable Wins 1937 Cape League Title In Spectacular Finish Monday

Barnstable won the 1937 Cape Cod title Monday morning in as spectacular a finish as the league has ever seen. Behind the flawless pitching of Norman Merrill the Barnstable team beat Bourne 5-0 to clinch the title. Had Bourne won the game, and followed up by beating Orleans in the afternoon, the title would have gone to the team from the Cape Cod Canal banks.

Not within anyone's memory has the Cape Cod league title been decided in such a marvelous finish. "Normie" sent Bourne away with no hits, no runs, and not even a passed batter. Only two of the opponents reached first base. It was the kind of a league finish which will go down in history. A good crowd turned out to see it, although not as large as it should have been. A high wind was blowing, but the sun was out most of the time.

Barnstable got going in the fourth, after three scoreless innings. Herman started things by getting a single. Pilote fanned but Giovannengeli was given a walk, putting Herman on second. Tominey drove one down to third which Moran tossed wildly, and Herman scored while Tominey reached first safely. O'Flaherty tapped a speedy one which Berry, the Bourne shortstop cleanly missed. It brought in Giovannageli and Tominey. Score, Barnstable three. In the fifth Vitale singled, and Colbert drove him across with a double. In the seventh Vitale scored again, getting home on Spinney's wild throw down to second, to catch Herman.

Barnstable Beats Bourne in Bunting Battle

500 fans paid admission to the High School field on Monday to see the crucial contest among the Championship Contenders. There should have been 5000 people present. The game was better than many a Major League classic.

* * * * * *

Ground Keeper "Jim" Anderson was on deck at 8:00 a.m., and rousing the association officials from their holiday slumbers to give him a hand at getting the rain soaked field into shape.

* * * * * *

Sand, Sawdust, and sweat, got the field in presentable condition by 10:30.

* * * * * *

It may have been football weath...

FINAL STANDING

	W	L	Pct.
Barnstable	29	17	.630
Harwich	27	19	.587
Bourne	26	19	.578
Falmouth	23	23	.500
Orleans	10	37	.213

Labor Day Games

Barnstable 5; Bourne 0
Orleans, 4; Bourne 0
Harwich 2, Falmouth 0
Harwich 3, Orleans 1

ever been displayed there since the grounds were laid out.

* * * * * *

The front page news in the *Hyannis Patriot* trumpets Norman Merrill's no-hitter against Bourne on the last day of the season which clinched the title for Barnstable. Reproduction courtesy of the *Barnstable Patriot.*

43

Apparently, the defeat sapped the spirits of the Bourne team. They dropped a 4–0 decision to lowly Orleans in the nightcap to fall into third place, behind Barnstable and Harwich.

The win gave Barnstable their third title in four years, and would place them alongside Falmouth (which would close out the ´30s having won five titles during the decade) as one of the teams of the decade. However, it would also mark the final Barnstable title, ending a dynasty. It is the ultimate tribute to Pete Herman and his players that they have been placed alongside the Orleans teams of the ´50s and the Cotuit teams of the ´60s and ´70s in the pantheon of great teams of the Cape Cod Baseball League.

· 4 ·

Shutdown and Renewal

"This is no proper time for amusements and entertainment for adults . . . This year we can very well dispense with baseball."
—Barnstable A.A. supporter John D.W. Bodfish at the March, 1945 Barnstable Town Meeting

For five long years, the Cape League was silent while America fought in World War II. Even among baseball people, there wasn't much of a debate on the subject. But that doesn't mean that the game died completely on the Cape. Several smaller, semipro leagues thrived, including many twilight circuits. One of the more popular leagues was the five-team Barnstable Recreation Commission Twilight League, which featured Barnstable, Hyannis, Osterville, Cotuit and West Hyannis. Players 18 years and under competed, while many of the older players went off to war.

But by the late ´40s, the Cape League began once again. Baseball fans, as well as the players, were excited about returning to the business of baseball on Cape Cod. However, there were a few changes in league policy: paid players were prohibited, and all players had to be "bona fide residents of Cape Cod." This was amended soon after to include all people with summer homes on the Cape, and, then again, to include all those who had summer jobs on the Cape.

It was the same situation for players as it had been before the

While World War II stopped the Cape League, that didn't mean
that baseball on the Cape stopped altogether. Chatham was
one of several towns, including many in and around
the Barnstable area, that continued to field teams.
Photo courtesy of Tom Desmond

war: town ballplayers made up the roster. But these players were usually more experienced than their pre-war counterparts. The 1947 Orleans team that ended up taking the championship had several players with some experience at the professional level. Pitcher Roy Bruninghaus remembers his team: "Left fielder Junie Lee had played pro ball by that time. I had a cup of coffee with the Canton Red Sox (a minor league affiliate of the Boston Red Sox), as well as catcher Red Eldredge and the Wilcox brothers, Buzzy and Stan. We were pretty experienced."

But attendance started to dwindle. Despite the nation's ravenous appetite for the major leagues, the Cape League started to suffer. In addition, the Cape League soon faced its first major competition when the Shenandoah League started play in 1947. Based in Staunton, Virginia, they had a 40-game schedule that ran from June until late July, and they attracted college stars from throughout the nation.

Back on the Cape, many teams were starting to slip through the cracks as the money dried up. In 1949, Sandwich, which is believed to have been the site of the first baseball game on the Cape in the 1860s, was faced with a dilemma. Only six young men were interested in playing on the town team. Shortly after, Sandwich ceased to field a baseball team at the highest level of competition on Cape Cod, and several of the players joined the fledgling Cotuit franchise.

That didn't mean that the level of play slipped appreciably among the top teams. The rivalries between the towns in the late '40s remained as fierce as ever. The epic battles between towns such as Orleans, Chatham, and Harwich remain legendary to this day. But even if the rest of the Cape was losing its interest in the Cape League, the players remained focused on the job at hand: winning baseball games.

In addition, the Cape was undergoing growing pains in the late '40s. Freed from travel restrictions such as gas rationing, tourists once again flooded the Cape during the summer months. Traffic became a major concern, and the Fourth of July congestion caused by tourists coming over the Sagamore and Bourne bridges was considered the worst in history by many.

"In the '30s, all we cared about was the girls," said Roy Bruninghaus, a member of both the pre- and post-World War II league, in a 1976 *Cape Cod Times* interview. "But after the war we had something to prove. The rivalries between the towns became bitter. Almost all of the players were locals and everybody knew everybody else."

"Before the modern day Cape League, it was a true town team," said longtime Yarmouth-Dennis player and coach Merrill "Red" Wilson. "When I first came to the Cape it was different. More people come to the games today than they ever did, but for the most part they just come and admire the game. There used to be a personal relationship there that seems to be lacking now. There were rivalries, but it was good-natured. When we went to Orleans, they also used to give us nicknames. When we went in there to play, it was always 'Hey, pretty boy.'"

Throughout the '50s, there were anywhere from 10 to 15 teams divided into two divisions, the Upper Cape and Lower Cape. In the Upper Cape were Sagamore, Otis AFB, Wareham, Falmouth, Barnstable (which played in Hyannis), Massachusetts Maritime and Cotuit. In the Lower Cape were Orleans, Eastham, North Truro, Harwich, Dennis, Yarmouth, Chatham and Brewster.

At that time, the league was primarily made up of Massachusetts natives, most of whom were Cape Codders who returned for the summer to play in the league that they helped build. Like the generations that came before them, a collection of teenagers, semipros and local college players filled the league.

The level of play was still above average, but baseball fans throughout the Cape began to get restless for the sparkling brand of baseball that seemed to dominate the league throughout the first part of the 20th century.

The local players filled positions admirably, but the league began to experience difficulties. Despite tourism reaching all-time highs, thanks to national recognition on many levels (Patti Page's 1957 musical smash "Old Cape Cod" certainly helped), attendance at games declined, people were giving less and less money when the hat was passed, and the league started to suffer. The league began staging promotions, such as the appearance of former Yankees like Eddie Lopat, Moose Skowron, Elston Howard and Phil Rizzuto at the 1960 all-star game.

But the rest of the Cape was on the move. In 1961, Cape Cod Community College was opened. Later that same year, the Cape Cod National Seashore was established, and would open to the public five years later. The Cape was moving forward financially, and as the '60s opened, one team was about to change the league forever with a fateful decision. As a result, baseball on Cape Cod would never be the same.

Under the headline "Strictly Amateur," a *Barnstable Patriot* story read: "Players from any college are eligible for the Cape Cod League this summer as it is to run on an amateur basis, but they will have to satisfy the college authorities in the fall that they had no remuneration if they wish to retain their amateur standing. This is the first time this has been permitted by most of the colleges, says President Thomas Otis." While the story was dated June 23, 1932, the real force of that announcement wouldn't hit the league for another 30 years. And appropriately enough, it was a team named the Clouters that would hit the league in a big way 30 years later.

The Sagamore team, frustrated over being relegated to the second division year after year, decided to take an important step. In the mid 50s, without giving notice to the rest of the league, they began actively recruiting the best college players throughout the nation. Lured by the promise of a summer of sun, fun, baseball and the possibility of being discovered by the ever-increasing number of professional scouts flocking to Cape Cod, most players took them up on the offer. Since there was no rule against it, many teams started doing the same thing, trying to keep up with the Clouters.

With Sagamore leading the way, the league began to become more and more competitive. The Clouters quickly became the class of the league. They took four titles in nine years, and while there were several key members of those clubs who were local players, such as the legendary pitcher Noel Kinski, most of the titles were won with help from outside talent. Soon, many other teams found ways of importing off-Cape players to enrich their rosters. And to legitimize those off-Cape players, many teams went to ridiculous extremes. Longtime Y-D coach Merrill "Red" Wilson recalls some chicanery that allowed several imports to become natives. "The league drew up some by-laws to allow imports—that's what they called them in those days," Wilson said. "But it got ridiculous after a while. They said you were a Cape native if you held property or paid taxes, so many of the teams would deed a piece of nondescript land to an imported ballplayer."

This sudden move toward bringing in imports often confused fans and teammates alike. A 1960 report in the *Patriot* said that it was okay to root for the hometown Barnstable Red Sox or the Cotuit Kettleers. "Don't feel confused if you can't recognize anyone. Don't worry about it—we are all in the same boat—even the local players themselves."

"The other teams began to see that if they wanted to compete, they would have to sign college players," said Arnold Mycock, Cotuit general manager.

The Sagamore club was led by Manny Robello, who would later go on to become the league's umpire-in-chief. "Manny began to bring in some real talent from off the Cape," Mycock remembered. "The Cleary brothers from Harvard, and Boston University pitcher Jim Powers and others. Before long, Sagamore was clobbering everybody else. This made us realize that we had to get going. First we went looking in the New England colleges, but before long everything was opened up and players started coming in from all over. They were getting jobs and living in boarding houses, much like today."

Sagamore may have begun the practice of importing players, but Arnold Mycock and the Cotuit Kettleers perfected the art of recruiting. While the players didn't exactly come from all across the country—many of them came from New England colleges such as Bowdoin, Bates, Holy Cross, and Boston College—they were still considered off-Cape talent.

Under first-year manager Jim Hubbard in 1961, the Kettleers won the first of four championships. The '64 team, in particular, was considered one of the most talented in league history. They posted a 31–3 mark, and seven of the players went on to play professional baseball.

With so much of the game in a constant state of flux on the Cape, several questions began to arise, including many about the state of umpiring. One problem that seemed to come up time and time again was just how much control an umpire had over the game. In the early 1960s, Joe Lombard was working the plate in a contest between Barnstable and Dennis. Lombard made a few close calls in favor of Dennis, and the Barnstable bench began to ride him unmercifully. He eventually lost patience with the bench jockeys, and ordered the Barnstable dugout cleared of all players save the nine men who were actually playing in the game and manager Ray Ellis.

The players then simply continued their baiting when they moved to the stands. The umpire then ordered them out of the stands. The players reluctantly moved a few feet back into the parking lot . . . and continued to ride the official.

Lombard then ordered them out of the parking area, as many Barnstable fans joined in the verbal fracas. The question then arose as to what the boundaries of the ballpark were, but cooler heads soon prevailed, and the game continued without incident.

As more and more of the best ballplayers in the country made their way to the Cape League throughout the early '60s, it soon became a more prestigious place to play for a New England ballplayer. As the caliber of play got better, many of the Northern schools were left behind because the poor weather prevented them from playing as many games as Southern schools. This gave Northern players fewer games, less practice, and cut down their chances of being seen by a professional scout even more.

Often, the local ballplayers who remained on Cape rosters grew resentful of others trying to crash the league that was built by and for Cape Cod boys. Many of the local ballplayers remain bitter to this day.

"Sure, there was resentment, which often showed up at town meetings," said longtime Yarmouth-Dennis coach Merrill "Red" Wilson. "I can only speak for Yarmouth and Dennis, but I know other towns where the towns started to cut back on the funding after imported ballplayers started coming in.

"When the radical change came, there was some resentment," Wilson continued. "I didn't see a lot of it in Yarmouth and Dennis, but I know that it happened in many communities. But it has been great for the Cape, and great for the towns, to be honest. We started to see a real high caliber of play since then."

"Every franchise still has to deal with that problem," said Jack Aylmer, who helped build the Bourne, Cotuit and Hyannis franchises and remains active in league matters. "The feeling on the part of a smattering of Cape Codders who have that buried resentment that it is not purely a 'Cape Cod League' anymore, but a mixture of college players.

"But I think that resentment isn't something that's building. I think it's waning, quite frankly, as a fuller appreciation of the Cape League exists."

CAPE BASEBALL SNAPSHOTS
1962: The Entrance into the Modern Era

In the fall of 1962, Chatham selectman and rabid baseball fan Robert A. McNeece started a project that would bring the Cape League into the modern age.

Along with other people like Jack Aylmer, he would meet at Judge Hudson's house on the Cape, and discuss how to keep the league financially secure. Throughout the '50s, it was clear that the league was hurting and often stumbled from year to year, hoping to make ends meet.

"He was just a real Cape Codder," recalled Aylmer. "He and his wife just loved the community and they were everywhere, all the time. He never seemed to disappear. He was always on Main Street, at Town Hall, or at the ballpark, where he always sat in the same place. He was probably the epitome of a good selectman, because whatever your problem, you could have a conversation about it with Bob."

McNeece was a big baseball fan, and knew how valuable a competitive Cape Cod Baseball League would be. A friend described him as a "little sliver of a man," who was a house painter and later got into politics.

"He was a nice, quiet man," said Tom Desmond, an acquaintance. "Oh, good lord, he was a big baseball man. And a wonderful organizer who later became president of the league."

Jack Aylmer helped build the Bourne, Hyannis, and Cotuit teams, worked with McNeece on several occasions in the early days of the league. "Bob was the guy who was the example," said Aylmer. "He was just a garden-variety selectman who loved baseball and loved Chatham. He was able to extract from the Chatham community the financial resources to keep Veteran's Park in shape, to install the first set of good lights.

"But it wasn't an easy job to raise $10,000 or $15,000 a year to keep a team on the field at that time. And Bob McNeece was able to do it the Cape Cod way, able to explain to Chatham residents the virtues of Cape League baseball and the advantages, businesswise, of having a family, leisure-time activity of having a team in your town. And everybody tried to emulate Bob McNeece, and that's why he's mentioned so often when it comes to the reorganization of the league, and Chatham became the league model when it came to raising money."

McNeece recognized that while relations between the Lower Cape and Upper Cape leagues were at a low, the two divisions needed each other. He knew that some action needed to be taken if the league were to survive. So, like the "good selectman" that he was, he brokered an agreement that would help take the league into the modern era.

"The two leagues fought amongst themselves," said longtime umpire Curly Clement. "The Upper Cape would say 'We'll play you when we feel like it.' And when it came to playoff time, they dictated who would play where and when, and would fight amongst themselves."

Despite a second straight championship by an exciting Cotuit team, fan support reached its lowest level that summer. A *Barnstable Patriot* story from the early '60s bemoaned the fact that "it is good to feel that the Cape once had a great league, which once turned out so many fine players and managers."

McNeece knew this, and gathered the most influential men in the Cape League at the home of Carter Whitcomb, a longtime Cotuit supporter. In attendance were McNeece, Whitcomb, Arnold Mycock (Cotuit general manager), Laurin "Pete" Peterson of Orleans, Merrill Doane (Chatham GM), Neil Mahoney (former Harwich manager and then Red Sox Director of Scouting) and Joe Sherman (sports editor of the *Cape Cod Times*, who once pitched for Connie Mack and the Philadelphia Athletics). They agreed that something should be done, and quickly.

Soon after that initial meeting, they met again and decided that a league commissioner was a necessity. On October 15, 1962, a 10-man committee plus a representative from Otis Air Force Base, which was to enter a team in the league, met at Otis. Joining them were various town officers, a representative from the Cape Cod Chamber of Commerce and a member of the Barnstable County Commissioners. More than 40 men in all were a part of the discussion regarding the future of baseball on Cape Cod.

The league executives agreed unanimously on a four-point plan that outlined the following:

1. Awarded the seven-man organization committee authority to nominate the league's first Commissioner to the acting Board of Directors.
2. Eliminated a league limit on outside, or off-Cape, players a team might use.
3. Set up a preliminary set of by-laws that outlined the initial organization of the new league.
4. Imposed an entrance fee of at least $500 on each member team, such fee to go toward salaries of umpires, scorers, and league officials.

The seven-man committee that would recommend the commissioner included Whitcomb, Mycock, Doane, Peterson, Sherman, George Karras (former president of the Upper Cape League) and Lowell Larson (former president of the Lower Cape League).

Less than a month later, and almost 42 years to the day that Major League Baseball named as their first commissioner Kenesaw Mountain Landis, the league Board of Directors met in the hearing room in the Barnstable Town Office Building. Eleven of the 12 teams were represented, and they were ready to move the Cape Cod Baseball League into the modern era.

They unanimously named a 66-year-old former professional baseball player and Cape native named Daniel J. Silva commissioner.

"In 1963, they decided that there was too much fighting between the leagues," said longtime umpire Curly Clement. "There were only eight teams, and that's when they decided to go with a commissioner. One commissioner, one boss. He would rule the roost. He's the one that put Cape Cod on the map. Danny Silva."

Despite news reports at the time, Silva was not the first commissioner of the league. A June 30, 1932 report in the *Hyannis Patriot,* headlined "Cape Baseball Czar," told the story of James Shepherd, the first baseball commissioner on the Cape: "James Shepherd of Chatham will be to the Cape Cod Baseball league what Judge Landis is to organized baseball as he was named high commissioner by the league at its meeting Wednesday night. This means he will be the final arbiter of all disputes as to players, dates and any other knotty problems that may arise during the season."

While Silva was the first commissioner of the modern era, his athletic exploits before coming to the Cape were impressive. He started with sports when he was in high school in Everett, picking up varsity letters in baseball and football from Everett High from 1913 through 1916, when he graduated. After high school graduation, he entered the Army. He was stationed at Camp Dix, New Jersey during World War I, and was the only man among the 50,000 troops to play three varsity sports—basketball, baseball, and football.

After the war ended, Silva continued his baseball career with the New England Baseball League for about a month before being called up to the Washington Senators. He stayed in the nation's capital until 1919, when he moved back to New England, this time with his old New England team in Fitchburg. He bounced around the minors for a couple of years before heading to the Cape and the fledgling Cape Cod League. He played and managed in the league from 1927 through 1932, and later managed Wareham (1927), Osterville (1928–30) and Barnstable (1931–32). He also served for a brief time as the umpire-in-chief of the Northern League, a well-respected counterpart to the Cape League.

Above: Former Chatham selectman Bob McNeece (left) was one of the most important people to help move the Cape League into the modern era in the 1960s.
Below: The CCBL named Danny Silva (left) its first commissioner almost 42 years to the day that the major leagues named Judge Kenesaw Mountain Landis their first commissioner. Photos courtesy of Arnold Mycock.

A beloved man who almost always wore a straw-boater in his later years, Silva had lived on the Cape full-time since early in 1948, when he moved back after a brief coaching stint with Honey Russell and the original Boston Celtics. He became an umpire with the Cape League in the ΄30s, and gained a small measure of renown as a fair and just arbiter. In fact, Silva's umpiring on the Cape was noted as far back as 1936, but the article in the *Hyannis Patriot* said that the impartial arbiters were "Tom Whalen and Danny Silver (*sic.*)"

Silva wasted no time in his new job. Just ten days after accepting the post, he named John DeMello of Falmouth and, in a nod to the man who helped put him there, Robert McNeece as his deputy commissioners. DeMello was to have control over the newly-formed Upper Cape Division, while McNeece was to oversee the Lower Cape Division.

As vital as McNeece was to the new league, DeMello was also important. He was known throughout Falmouth, and managed the Falmouth team for many years, in addition to serving as a high school basketball referee. The Falmouth selectman attended the first meeting at Otis, and had been solidly behind the new plan since its inception.

"I feel confident these men will do an excellent job as we attempt to rebuild the Cape Cod Baseball League to the prominence it once enjoyed," Silva said in an interview with the *Cape Cod Times* soon after assuming the post of commissioner. "Each is well-qualified in his particular field and will be a valuable part of the team which will oversee the operation of the league. I take particular pride in announcing the acceptances of Mr. DeMello and Mr. McNeece, two public officials who have consented to work baseball into their already busy schedules," he continued.

Silva also appointed John Hinckley of Hyannis, president of John Hinckley and Sons Lumber Company, one of the Cape's biggest companies, the secretary-treasurer of the league, and Joseph Sherman, sports editor of the *Cape Cod Standard-Times,* the league statistician. Like his two other choices, both Sherman and Hinckley already had a long association with the league. Sherman had served as chief statistician for the old Upper Cape League the year before. Hinckley was a well-known businessman who helped out the Barnstable club, and was a noted football official.

On June 17, 1963, the Cape League stepped into the modern age. With the merger of the Upper Cape and Lower Cape leagues into one, unified Cape Cod Baseball League, the teams were as follows: in the Upper Division, Wareham, Bourne, Sagamore, Falmouth, and Cotuit faced each other; in the Lower Division, it was Otis Air Force Base, Yarmouth, Chatham, Orleans and Harwich. Each team had a 34-game schedule, the most extensive in league history.

On the eve of the first Opening Day to be presided over by the new commissioner, anticipation was rampant. Some big-time collegiate all-stars had signed on for the 1963 season, including "Cotton" Nash. An All-American who also starred in basketball at the University of Kentucky, Nash joined the Cotuit team. That week, Silva was interviewed by the *Cape Cod Standard-Times:*

> "We hope to build the new league into a top notch outfit like the old Cape League which sent so many players to the Majors," said Silva. "Fellows like Lenny Merullo, Shanty Hogan, Red Rolfe and Johnny Broaca got their start here. There's no reason we can't give other promising players the same opportunity."

PART II

Onward and Upward:
1963–Present

· 5 ·

Growing Pains: The 1960s

"My summer on Cape Cod (1966) was the best summer I ever had in baseball, bar none. I was there for two months, and there is nothing more beautiful than the Cape in the summertime. The league was a great league, and I just can't say enough good things about it."

— Former Texas Rangers player and GM Tom Grieve

Shortly after naming Danny Silva its first commissioner of the modern era in 1963, the Cape League hoped to include itself in the newly-formed National Collegiate Baseball Federation (NCBF). This organization acted as the forerunner to the NCAA as the governing body of summer collegiate baseball leagues. Allying itself with the NCBF would have two advantages: First, the Cape League would receive the national recognition and merit that had always eluded it; second, it would avail the league a sizable amount of grant money that the NCBF doled out every year to the summer leagues.

Founded in 1962 by J. Walter Shannon, Midwestern director of scouting for the Cleveland Indians, and J. Robert Stewart, Athletic Director at St. Louis University, the NCBF had a broad goal. Their aim was "to encourage, collaborate on and with, foster, promote and advance amateur baseball in the U.S. for those of college age, so as to provide training and instruction and recreation for such young people, particularly during the months when school is not in session."

The NCBF was very active in the creation of summer collegiate leagues throughout the nation. It was no secret that the federation had plans to expand its program of summer leagues, with the eventual aim being four major summer college circuits — one on the East Coast, one in the West, and two others somewhere in between.

To this end, 1963 was the first season of the Central Illinois Collegiate League. Developed by the federation, it received the support and endorsement of the Major Leagues through Commissioner Ford Frick's office, as well as the NCAA and the United States Baseball Federation.

Compared to the Cape League, the Central Illinois Collegiate League was extremely well-funded — over $100,000 in two years from a variety of sources throughout organized baseball — and well-run, with strong local support. It had clubs in Springfield, Galesburg, Peoria, Bloomington, Lincoln and Champaign, and featured a top-notch brand of baseball. It still runs very well today, with teams in Champaign, Decatur, Danville, Fairview Heights, Springfield, and Twin City. Former players include Mike Schmidt, Kirby Puckett, and Jeff Fassero. More than 150 of their former players have gone on to the major leagues.

The Cape, while not admitting it openly, had become jealous of the attention as well as the money the new league was getting. They hoped to even the score the following spring.

On March 9, 1965, word came down that the NCAA had certified nine leagues, including the Cape League. This meant that the players in the nine summer college circuits were free to compete without jeopardizing their amateur status. It was also understood that these nine leagues were to receive most of the $75,000 that major league baseball had allocated for summer college baseball.

However, no announcement was made outright because the NCBF was in the process of moving their offices from St. Louis to Kansas City. A spokesman said that no allocation of funds would be made until the new articles of incorporation were filed for the organization. It would turn out to be a fatal postponement for the Cape League.

With the understanding that it would be receiving a sizable grant, the Cape League had planned an ambitious 42-game schedule, with baseball play stretching the entire length of Cape Cod all summer. Commissioner Silva remained upbeat.

"We operated long before any foundation existed," he said defiantly. "And we will operate again this season."

"Sure, we could have used the money," he continued. "But let's see what the future brings. Right now, we will be concentrating on a first-class league this summer."

The Cape League turned their focus inward. Despite the lack of anticipated funds from the NCBF, they concentrated on becoming the premier summer college league by starting to recruit players from around the nation. Their efforts began to pay off for the first time in 1964 when Cotuit pitcher Keith Weber and Orleans outfielder Brian Edgerly were lured from the Cape to play on the U.S. National Team, which played an exhibition schedule in Japan before competing in the Olympics. They soon began attracting some of the top-flight young managers.

"It was around that time that the league began to attract younger managers," said former league PR chief Dick Bresciani. "Dave Gavitt, Lou Lamoriello, Joe Lewis, Jr., Tony Williams. Guys who were younger, more enthusiastic, and started to aggressively go out and look for better players. They had a real top-notch group of managers, with guys like Bill Livesey."

They also began work on improving the umpiring. Soon after Silva was named commissioner, the umpires began dealing directly with the single league office, making things considerably easier. Paperwork, assignments and paychecks came directly from the league. At that time, umpires were getting a flat per-game fee from the league, plus a cut of whatever was collected from fans at the game. Longtime umpire Curly Clement remembers how the system worked:

> "At that time, in the Cape Cod League, they used to pass the hat around," Clement said. "The plate umpire got the bills, and the base umpire got all the change. I used to come home with a pocketful of nickels and dimes and pennies."

But Silva saw to it that the umpires were well paid.

"Umpires will be paid twice a month, on the first and the 15th, exactly as is done in organized ball," Silva promised in 1963. "In this way, there will be no squabbles with individual teams. All paperwork will be handled through the league office."

Silva, a former umpire in the now defunct Northern League, hired and assigned the umpires. They began working in teams, as in the major leagues. The first eight umpires hired were John McGinn, Cal Burlingame, Marty McDonough ("One of the best college umpires and college football umpires I had ever seen," said Clement. McDonough was also a top-flight second baseman for Harwich in the early days of the league.), John Tambolleo, Roger Scudder, Manny Pena (the father-in-law of former Boston first baseman George Scott, according to Clement), Curly Clement, and George Murphy ("A big, heavyset guy," Clement recalls. "As slow as an elephant. But one of the best ball and strike men I've ever seen. You get him on the bases and he was lost.").

While the umpires had to be tough to survive, Clement recalled that McGinn was tougher than most.

"He used to chew tobacco," Clement said. "And he used to come over after the ballgame, and he would chew my butt out, swear at me, spit all over me. I would get home and sit down and cry. I was so down-hearted."

Silva assured them that they had complete control over the game. "Our umpires will be the best we can get," continued Silva. "They will dress and act like professionals, and I'm sure that they will do an outstanding job."

"Danny Silva was tough but fair," Clement recalled, who began umpiring in the Cape League in 1961. "He used to say to us: 'You're getting paid to umpire: dress like an umpire. I don't want you to come in with an old hat. I don't want to see you come to the ballpark and have soup stains or chewing tobacco on your shirt. I want your shoes shined. I want you to have clean clothes, clean pants. Look like an umpire. You're getting paid for it. Look professional.'"

On March 9, 1965, it was announced that the NCAA had certified nine leagues. Besides the Cape League, the following summer

Above: Cotuit players gather at one of the Yankee Stadium monuments in the early 1970s. All-Star Games between the CCBL and the Atlantic Collegiate Baseball League were held at Yankee Stadium and Fenway Park, with occasional forays to Veteran's Stadium in Philadelphia or Shea Stadium in New York.
Below: The 1983 contest was held at Fenway. Cape Leaguers pose in front of Fenway's famed left field wall.
Photos courtesy of Arnold Mycock and Jack Aylmer.

leagues were certified: Shenandoah Valley, Midwest College, Central Illinois Collegiate, Basin, Kentucky — Indian, St. Louis, Baseball Summer League of the Mid-South, and the Northwest League. In addition, four independent teams received certification: teams in Junction, Colorado; Fairbanks, Alaska; Liberal, Kansas; and Seattle-Tacoma, Washington.

Late in the summer of 1965, the league became a corporation in the eyes of the state. Secretary of the Commonwealth Kevin White (who would later go on to serve as the Mayor of Boston in the '70s) issued the charter, which stated:

"Now, therefore, I, Kevin H. White, Secretary of the Commonwealth of Massachusetts, do hereby certify that said Daniel J. Silva (commissioner), Stephen C. Robbins (Wareham), Arnold W. Mycock (Cotuit), Joseph C. Gavin (Harwich), Kenneth G. Clarke, Jr. (Sagamore), David B. Willard (Orleans), Merrill T. Doane (Chatham), Carlos Pena (Falmouth), Richard T. Welch (Yarmouth), their associates and successors are legally organized and established as, and are hereby made an existing corporation as of July 30, 1965 under the name Cape Cod Baseball League, Inc. with the powers, rights and privileges, and subject to the limitations, duties and restrictions, which by law appertain thereto."

The new parameters of the league were as follows: championship games were no longer played on Labor Day weekend, because the college students had to return to school. With the Upper and Lower Cape divisions now established, regular season games were to be played within the division only to limit travel. In addition, the number of scheduled games was increased to offset the dwindling number of playoff games.

A year later, the annual grant from the NCBF was increased to $5,000. Each team's schedule was increased from 34 to 40 games. At the league meeting in Hyannis that February, the decision was made to pare the rosters to 18 players, including four "non-college" players, none of whom could be more than 24 years old.

The $5,000 grant allowed for many things, including a raise for umpires (from $10 to $12 a game), employing official scorers at every Cape League contest, and providing each team with 10 dozen brand new baseballs and three dozen new wooden bats at the start of every year.

Other summer college leagues soon took root throughout the country. The Atlantic Collegiate Baseball League (ACBL), based in Park Ridge, New Jersey, started in the mid-60s. Games ran from June through August, and eight teams operated in the New York, New Jersey and Pennsylvania area. In addition, the six-team Central Illinois Collegiate League opened for business in 1963 in Bloomington, providing another outlet for summer college talent throughout the Midwest.

Soon after the ACBL began, the idea of an all-star game between the Cape Leaguers and the newly formed circuit was broached by a collegiate baseball coach from New York. It would be another three years before such a game would take place, but the idea had been planted.

St. John's University head baseball coach Jack Kaiser, who was friendly with both the Yankees and the Mets, suggested an all-star game to be played at either Yankee Stadium or Shea Stadium. The game would be played on a Monday night sometime in midsummer, and both teams could enjoy the thrill of playing in a major league ballpark.

Even in their relative infancy as a league, the CCBL was supremely confident about the outcome of the proposed all-star game.

"It would be no contest," Arnold Mycock said. "I can't see any way they could possibly beat an all-star team from our league. This would give us an excellent opportunity to prove just how strong we are."

That series did eventually come to pass, and Mycock's pronouncement wasn't far from the truth. The Cape League All-Stars would face an all-star squad from the ACBL for the first time in 1970, in a contest at Yankee Stadium. The two teams would oppose each other every year until 1987, with the Cape League finishing up the series with an impressive 13–2–1 edge over their ACBL counterparts.

In 1968, Silva stepped aside as commissioner and former Cotuit pitcher Bernie Kilroy was named the new leader of the CCBL.

Kilroy was perhaps best known for throwing a no-hitter for the Kettleers against Massachusetts Maritime in 1961, allowing just one walk. In 1969, he oversaw the merger of the Upper and Lower Cape divisions to form a single, eight-team league. Now, there were clubs in Chatham, Cotuit, Falmouth, Harwich, Hyannis, Orleans, Wareham, and Yarmouth.

Things were changing for the Cape League. Players had to work, as the NCAA soon stated that regardless of a player's ability or professional prospects, the rules were the same for everyone: "Only freshmen, sophomores and juniors having baseball eligibility remaining may play in a certified summer league which receives a grant of $10,000 or more. Further, no team shall have more than four players from one college. These athletes *must* be offered the opportunity to be gainfully employed in a real and necessary job. Compensation paid to such athletes for work performed must be commensurate with the going rate of that locale for service of like character, and shall be given for services actually performed."

As a result, Buck Showalter worked a lunch counter in Hyannis in the summer of 1976. Frank Thomas worked mowing lawns on Brewster Green in 1988. Jeff Bagwell washed dishes at Friendly's in Chatham in 1987. In 1988, Mo Vaughn painted houses in Wareham. Erik Hanson did landscaping in Harwich during the summer of 1984. And in 1987, Robin Ventura worked at Puritan Clothing in Hyannis. It didn't matter how good you were or where you came from — you had to work at a job during the regular season if you wanted to make money.

While some ballplayers today have the financial wherewithal to get by without a job, the tradition of working ballplayers dates back all the way to the early days of the 20th century.

"Players could not support themselves through baseball alone," said Tod Owen, who played for one of the several Falmouth club teams from 1907 through 1911. "They did provide jobs for the fellas, but they did make them work. Mostly, they worked for the town cutting grass, and they would work on the roads."

Many of the players today come from high-profile collegiate environments, where they are pampered and treated like superstars. But in the Cape League, even the superstars aren't above taking jobs washing dishes, painting houses or manicuring the field. That doesn't mean that they all enjoy it. Jack Aylmer recalls running into Ron Perry, Jr.'s father during Ron's MVP campaign in the Cape League in 1979.

"He came up to me with his son and said 'Look at these blisters on his hands!'" Aylmer recalls. "'How did he get these?' I think Ronny was doing some landscaping work that summer.

"I told him that's what the Cape League is all about. It's work, and rent, and food and travel and a job."

"This isn't like the Pac-10, or one of the big football conferences, where these guys have students' jobs like 'Your job is to turn on the automatic sprinklers that go on by themselves'" noted Steve Buckley of the *Boston Herald.* "A lot of these guys have real jobs. They're washing dishes and making beds and stuff like that. That again brings up the grassroots aspect of the Cape Cod League."

"I worked at a local country market in Cotuit," remembers Anaheim's Tim Salmon, who played for the Kettleers in 1988. "I was the clerk at the front, and made sandwiches at the deli. It was great."

However, it wasn't always this way. In the '20s and '30s, the players made their money from playing baseball. In Depression-era America, this was an ideal job for any red-blooded young American man.

"In the '20s and '30s, we didn't have to work," recalled Bill Carpenter in a 1976 interview in the *Cape Cod Times.* Carpenter played for Falmouth in 1935. "Our job was to play baseball, and we got paid for doing that."

"I got $15 a week with room and board," Bill Gallagher said in the same article. He pitched with the Barnstable Red Sox during the early '30s. "And $10 for every game I won, and that wasn't bad."

But as the league entered the modern era with more collegians, the NCAA dictated that the players had to start showing up for work in the morning if they wanted to get paid. As the league entered the modern era, the word quickly spread: if you were playing in the Cape League, you should get to the Cape early to get the best and easiest jobs. Texas Rangers broadcaster Tom Grieve played for Chatham in 1966, but got to the Cape later than most of his team.

"I worked for Walter V. Love as a painter," recalled Grieve with a smile. "I got there late, and all the good jobs had been taken. Everyone else had the nice jobs as a lifeguard and that sort of thing. Meanwhile, I got to the ballpark at 5:30 every day with paint all over myself and tireder than hell, and I had to play a ballgame that night. But I loved it."

In the early days, however, the jobs quite often interfered with the game. A hot summer afternoon in 1956 provided Y-D manager Merrill "Red" Wilson with a lesson in what it takes to be a good volunteer fireman. Wilson recalls:

"One afternoon, we were playing at Simkins Field. John Sears was playing centerfield. Right in the middle of the game, the fire whistle blew, and Sears took off for his car. He was a volunteer fireman, and I was left looking for a centerfielder the rest of the afternoon.

"Well, a few days later we had another game, and I made sure I talked to John beforehand. I said 'John, I just didn't understand what you did the other day. I can appreciate the fact that you are a volunteer firefighter, but why did you take off so quickly without telling anyone?'

"He answered 'If it was your house that was on fire, you'd have wanted me to leave just as fast.'"

"Buck Showalter worked at a breakfast and luncheon store in Hyannis, the Hyannis News Store," said Hyannis's Jack Aylmer, who housed him and helped get him his job. "He used to get up at five o'clock in the morning, and go over and flip eggs and bacon."

"What did I take away from my experience in the Cape Cod League?" asks Mike Pagliarulo, who played for Chatham in 1980. "I learned to clean the city of Chatham real well because I worked for the town there."

"Do you have any idea how little I know about ice hockey?" Robin Ventura told the *Barnstable Patriot* in a 1996 interview. The Oklahoma State product worked at the sporting goods department in Puritan Clothing in Hyannis during the summer of 1987. "Every time someone would come in looking for help with new skates

Ronnie Perry, Jr. was a collegiate baseball and basketball star
at Holy Cross, but his father wasn't ready for the idea of his
working at a summer job while playing in the Cape League.
Photo courtesy of Jack Aylmer

or other equipment, I'd have to find another sales associate to assist me."

"I worked more than anyone else on our team and got paid less money," recalled Bob Tewksbury, who threw for Wareham in 1980. "I was a grounds crew guy for the field, and the guy that brought me back and forth to work every day, Rob Murphy, made more money than I did, and I worked 40 hours a week."

Boston Red Sox third baseman Tim Naehring painted houses in Barnstable the summer of 1987.

"It was quite the experience," Naehring recalls. "Being afraid of heights, for one. I was going up on the second and third floors, painting houses. I also got to find out how many little wooden schoolhouses there were in the town of Barnstable. I think I painted all of them for about four dollars an hour."

"I worked at the A & P deli in Chatham," said Anaheim's Gary DiSarcina, who played for Harwich in 1987. "I sliced meat. I don't know if that was a real smart job for a baseball player. You've got to use your hands a lot, and I used a slicer. I cut my fingernails short a couple of times."

"The job situation changes from year-to-year," said Y-D GM Jim Hagemeister. "The jobs run between five dollars and eight dollars. We try not to say, 'Hey, this kid comes from a top program. We'll give him the best job.' It doesn't work out that way."

Almost every team's photo guide has an announcement thanking local merchants for giving players jobs, and most local businesses are asked in the off season to help provide jobs for ballplayers.

However, a lucky few ballplayers get jobs working at the team clinics, which offer baseball instruction to kids. All 10 franchises offer them, but Cotuit was the first. In 1975, Cotuit's Jack McCarthy initiated the Kettleers' clinic for kids between the ages of eight and twelve years old. Since their inception, thousands of kids have received guidance and support in pursuit of a possible career in baseball. The clinics are available to all residents and summer visitors, usually with one session in the morning and one in the afternoon.

Robin Ventura had trouble fitting customers with ice skates
while working at Puritan's Clothing Store of
Hyannis during the summer of 1987.
Photo courtesy of Jack Aylmer.

In the pre-World War II era, Cape Cod players would stay together at a hotel or boarding house. It was a good way for management to keep an eye on the team and was an excellent idea so far as the Harwich clubs of the mid-30s were concerned. According to a 1983 article in the *Cape Cod Times* by former player Til Ferdenzi, they weren't always the most talented team on the field, but they always managed to have more fun than most. They would stay at the Harwich Inn at the corner of Parallel and Bank Streets, but spent most of their free time at Jacob's Garden, just over the Chatham line on Route 28.

While at Jacob's Garden, commonly known as Jake's, second baseman Marty McDonough would entertain the team with his own rendition of the tune "It's June in January." However, after a glass or two of Hanley's Ale, which cost 35 cents a quart, the singing would become infinitely better. On amateur nights at Jake's, McDonough almost always took first prize, which was $5. According to Ferdenzi, it almost always went for beer for his teammates.

When it came time to retire for the evening, the players would return to the Harwich Inn. Washing up was a challenge, as the 15 or so ballplayers shared one bathroom with one shower and one tub.

Meals would be eaten at the Mulcays, which some Harwich historians may recognize as Bob Winston's old Sunoco station. There were rarely complaints about the cooking, which was handled three times a day by the elder Mrs. Mulcay. One day, an unfortunate rookie decided to send his scrambled eggs back to the kitchen, saying "My mother never cooked scrambled eggs this way."

Mrs. Mulcay replied, "Eggs is eggs."

"That was the last time he heard anyone complain about Mrs. Mulcay's food," Ferdenzi said.

As the years progressed, teams found it easier and cheaper to place the players with local families in the community. Records indicate that this practice may have started in the 1930s, when, as a cost-cutting measure, the Barnstable club considered placing them throughout the town: "It is proposed to get people such as restaurants and boarding houses to take the players for board on the idea of full board $8 for one with no charge for a second player," stated the July 20, 1933 article in the *Hyannis Patriot*.

But many realized that the idea of placing players with local townsfolk created in a player a sense of pride in that town, and made him feel that he was not only playing for the town, but for the people he was living with.

However, there were sometimes exceptions to the rule. During the 1967 season, the entire Orleans team stayed at what used to be known as Sands Cottages, located across the street from Eldredge Park. Coincidentally enough, it was located right next to the police station, which was convenient if a player or two happened to run into trouble with the law.

Along with several on-field changes, the '60s saw the start of many players living as boarders in the community. Today, it is usually at a cost of $40 to $50 a week. Local families welcome college players into their homes, and are responsible for his room and board. As a result, some lasting relationships develop.

Jeremy and Susan Gilmore of Barnstable have hosted Cotuit ballplayers for many years. They told the *Boston Globe* in an interview in February 1995 that the relationships that develop make things special for the volunteers who open their homes.

"That's a thrill for volunteers, of course, seeing kids make it to the big leagues and being able to say 'I knew them when,'" Gilmore said. He counts Tim Salmon and Tim Naehring as former boarders with whom he has maintained relationships over the years.

"You don't set up this stipend to make money," Gilmore said. "If you do, I think you're missing the point. If you really do it conscientiously, you spend a lot more money than you receive, but that's okay. They're your kids for the summer, you do what you have to do. But there are some people who feel that if there is no money, there is no food, and that's ridiculous."

Not all living situations are perfect, according to Wareham assistant general manager John Claffey. "There are players that don't connect, and it's not always the player's fault," Claffey said. "There are some people who want to house players that shouldn't house players. They say 'Boy, I want to house one of these guys because they could become a big league player.' But they end up clashing with the player that stays with them for whatever reason."

"I'm afraid the motivation for a lot of people is for a playmate for their child," said Barbara Ellsworth. By the late '90s, she had housed 69 players over the years in both the Harwich and Y-D teams. "They don't realize that today's college kid usually doesn't have time to be a playmate, to teach baseball to a seven-year-old, because they work so hard. They play 44 games. They want to see some of the Cape, have some sort of social life."

· 6 ·

The Modern Era Begins

"There's just something short of wonderful about Cape Cod base-ball, but then — if we are to believe Henry David Thoreau and/or Patti Page — there's something just short of wonderful about Cape Cod." — Sports Illustrated writer Steve Wulf in 1981

Former league commissioner and president Dick Sullivan believes that the early days of the league inspired a town loyalty that was hard to shake once the off-Cape players began playing in the CCBL in the '60s and '70s.

"I think that with the long history of the Cape League, the town teams were very big," Sullivan said. "In the early days of the league, there were great fan loyalties among the townspeople, following their boys from town to town. It would be a happening, an outing, when Orleans would play Chatham. Everybody would pack a lunch and go down to Orleans on Sunday afternoon and vice-versa.

"So to the young men who lived in these smaller towns, local town baseball and town loyalty were very important. The loyalty developed through representation of their local athletic teams, whether it was the town team or high school level. And a lot of people who have lived on the Cape for many years have retained that feeling. When the high-caliber talent came in from all parts of the country, they were out-of-towners, off-Cape people, so it took

Former league president and commissioner Dick Sullivan
(right) was one of several league officials who tried to
merge the local players with imported talent as the
league changed in the late 1960s and early 1970s.
Photo courtesy of Jack Aylmer.

awhile for some of the towns to get adjusted to a new form, a new sense of ownership."

But the majority of newspapers soon became resigned to the fact that the Cape League was inching closer and closer to an all-collegiate league, devoid of local talent. The *Cape Cod Times* stated in 1964 that "the local players should not be discouraged from competing, but the better the competition, the more fans will turn out. Obviously, there is no community on Cape Cod which could field an all-local team and provide a winner that fans would support." Later in that same story, local teams that had tried to field an all-Cape lineup and failed were listed. They included Sagamore and Falmouth, which quickly turned to recruiting outside help when they found that they were being badly outplayed.

"A lot of the kids who played in local baseball around here kind of resented the college kids coming in and getting the limelight," said local pitcher Mike Rainnie, who pitched for Falmouth from 1969 through 1971. "There were only a few local kids who were asked to play. There were three kids on our team that were asked to play, and we didn't play much, because we had an excellent team. I don't know if it was resentment. But I know the kids who were recruited in the early days definitely had a funny feeling, a strange welcome from the Cape League coming down here."

And some of that resentment stretched into the media coverage. With the number of local players on the wane in the 1960s, the backlash against "outsiders" became apparent when the league was relegated to the back pages of the paper, with less and less coverage. Whereas the league often received front-page coverage in papers such as the *Barnstable Patriot* in the ´20s, ´30s and ´40s, it was now given short shrift, usually with only a brief mention. CCBL accounts competed with the work of local columnists such as Hartley Davis, who wrote "Sports with Rod & Gun" for the *Patriot,* and it was left to the real old-timers to remember the days when the Cape turned out some real major leaguers.

But there were still some columnists who extolled the virtues of the Cape League, no matter where the players came from. In a 1962 essay in the *Dennis-Yarmouth Register,* Hadyn Mason said he still believed that the Cape League was his favorite brand of baseball:

> "Maybe I'm not what you'd call a real baseball fan because, as far as I am concerned, all the palaver about the Red Sox leaves me cold. As a matter of fact, anyone who wants can hustle themselves up to Boston hoping to see a no-hit, no-run game. That's not for me . . . I like a game that isn't a 'money-sport,' but one in which the players are working their heads off because they love the game. That's why I'm such a push-over for our local town team and the Lower Cape League. The home-folks men, plus some college talent, put on a show that has plenty of excitement. If you don't see these games and if you don't follow the standing of the team, you are missing a lot of good baseball and a lot of good, wholesome entertainment . . . It is surprising what home-town support does for these players who are doing their best to produce. Let's give it to them."

But while many local players seemed to be on the outs, several local managers remained safe in their positions. The idea of college coaches for college ballplayers was broached as early as 1964, when the first imported college players arrived on the scene. However, based on the success of managers such as Jim Hubbard in Cotuit and Steve Robbins in Wareham, Commissioner Danny Silva felt that the local managers had earned the right to be where they were.

"If Steve Robbins left Wareham, there would be no team there," Silva told the *Cape Cod Times* in a 1964 interview. "And how can you question the ability of Jim Hubbard at Cotuit? He's won four straight pennants."

But the *Cape Cod Times* seemed to waffle on the idea later in the same story. While they praised the results that Hubbard and Robbins had obtained, they surmised that if the league were to go all-college in their player selection, they should do the same when they selected coaches.

"Hubbard has earned the right to continue at the helm of the Kettleers as long as he and the Cotuit A.A. see fit, and Robbins has practically singlehandedly kept the Wareham franchise alive for 30-odd years, frequently with title-contending teams.

"But we still believe there is a definite need to bring more good baseball men into the Cape League.

"To get these men, money must be made available. Top college coaches would jump at the opportunity to spend a summer on Cape Cod if they were paid. This, Cape League officials believe, could be done through the (NCBF). But then, all managers would have to meet the foundation's qualifications."

The last part was the key sticking point that perhaps led to this proposal's downfall. Despite the increased money that was coming in from the NCBF, the Cape League still wanted to maintain some sense of independence. It was here that many locals took a stand, and, as a result, local managers stayed in control of most ball clubs until the 1980s and beyond.

As local players began to give way to more talented off-Cape players, a certain confusion developed for the fans who had followed their hometown team for years. Witness this exchange in June of 1960, as detailed in the *Barnstable Patriot*:

"If you are a typical Barnstable Red Sox or Cotuit Kettleers fan and have watched these teams in one of the first games, you probably were favorably impressed by the caliber of the players but feel confused because you don't recognize hardly anybody.

"Don't worry about it—we are all in the same boat—even the players themselves.

"We weren't able to watch the Red Sox Monday night so Tuesday morning we asked their third baseman, Georgie Williams, how the game had gone.

"Georgie detailed some of the pertinent facts about how Doug Higgins had pitched a no-hitter, that the team had backed him up with some stout hitting, including a pinch hit home run.

"'Who belted that?' we inquired.

"'Don't ask me,' Georgie replied. 'He was some new guy I never laid eyes on before that night.'

"As we say, it is confusing. One possible out would be to

have the players wear shirts with their names on the back, like the Chicago White Sox.

"Only thing is, in order for it to be much help they also should carry the name of the college or whatever they play for regularly — and that lettering job would run into real money."

"This is your team, and you will find that Yarmouth will be playing more local boys than most other teams," said Yarmouth Indians business manager Dick Welch in an interview prior to the 1963 season. Despite an impassioned belief in local talent, Yarmouth finished the season with a 7–24 mark. Soon after, the Indians began recruiting players.

But Falmouth's Mike Rainnie attributed the success of the Commodores to the local players on their roster in the late '60s and early '70s when they would win four straight titles.

"I think one of the things that helped the team come together was the fact that we did have some local boys on the team that bridged the gap and helped the visiting players feel more a part of the community," Rainnie said. "They would have questions about where to go or what to do, and we were able to tell them what was going on."

And it remains true today that if a Cape Cod youngster, or any young man from eastern Massachusetts, is good enough, he will be selected. For many of them, it remains a special opportunity to play in front of the home folks.

"Going to school in Miami, I was away from home," said Medford, Massachusetts native Mike Pagliarulo, who played shortstop for Chatham in 1980. "Playing on the Cape provided me a chance for some of my relatives, who I care a lot about, to come and see me play a game that I love. It worked out real well, and I was real glad that I did it."

"I think it was a little more special because I was a local guy," said Canton, Massachusetts native Bobby Witt, who pitched for Chatham in 1983. "Being not too far from your home, the family could come down there and watch you play. It was exciting, and I really enjoyed it."

Former Barnstable High pitcher Peter Princi is one of the few locals who has enjoyed recent success at the CCBL level. After spending the season at Wake Forest, he returned to the Cape to help the 1995 Hyannis Mets as a reliever.

"Princi's going to be good," Hyannis manager Steve Mrowka told the *Cape Cod Times* in the early 1995 season. "He's got a good arm. What he needs is some experience, and to work on consistency with his off-speed stuff. We didn't keep him on the team because he's a local boy. We kept him on the team to help us win."

Princi, who returned for a second season in 1996, is often cast as the last of the Cape Cod players who can compete at the CCBL level. He says that he doesn't mind being a symbol for Cape natives.

"I get a little bit of that, but in a way it's kind of nice," Princi said in a 1996 interview. "It really makes me play harder. It's nice getting that kind of attention."

Princi also counts himself lucky that his parents can see him play.

"Most of the kids' parents come to the Cape for a week or two, but I think it's a little more special for me," he said. "It's where I grew up, where I went to the games, and I've always loved the Cape Cod game."

"For years, the New England scouts have been pushing to get more New England kids (in the CCBL), because the ones that come here hold their own," said former Seattle Mariners scout Jack Webber. "But a lot of the clubs seem to gravitate towards the Sun Belt kids, along with the high-profile schools, which is natural. So other venues like the new New England Collegiate Baseball League, based in Connecticut, will provide some more opportunities for New England kids."

Many of the local ballplayers who hung around in the late '60s still recall their association with some of the future major leaguers who would help make the Cape League recognizable around the baseball world. Orleans native John Mayo played in the Cape League as a teenager in the '50s, and left to serve in the U.S. Marine Corps. When he returned to play for Orleans in the early '60s, he was 24 years old. He wasn't a wide-eyed teenager any more, but was still awed by the sight of a young catcher from the University of New Hampshire—Carlton Fisk.

"That was the year we were playing at the Orleans Middle School field because they were re-doing Eldredge Park," Mayo recalled in a 1994 interview in the *Cape Codder*. "I'll never forget it. You could tell right away that he had it, a catcher with a rocket for an arm. They didn't have a fence, and he would hit these line drives that would roll a mile."

In 1967, teams were limited to 18-man rosters, with only four non-college (meaning local) players, none of whom could be more than 24 years old. It was the last year for Mayo, who was 27 years old at the time.

"It was a good caliber of a league even before the college players got there," Mayo recalled. "It's just a nice memory to have."

It was only a matter of time until the local players were phased out entirely. In 1970, the NCAA increased the annual grant to $10,000, and handed down the rule that all players must be collegians. The era of the town team was over. While the league didn't place a sign out front saying "No Locals Need Apply" in 1970, many Cape natives interpreted it that way.

"I remember my first year (1971), I took all these New England players on the word from their coaches, and I ended up dead last," said Fred Ebbett in a 1987 interview in the *Cape Cod Times*. "The league was changing them. It was expanding along the East Coast and into Florida."

But that wasn't the only problem that many longtime league officials faced. Some friendships were torn asunder as a result of the change in league policy, never to be the same again.

"[The local players] resented it very much," said former Cotuit GM Arnold Mycock. "I know lots of former players wouldn't have anything to do with our league after it was announced."

"I was against the idea of importing players," said Wally Raneo, who was a local ballplayer with Harwich and the Cape Verdeans in the '40s and '50s. "Of course, being a local guy myself, I was a little biased."

Mycock had been the Cotuit GM since the 1950s, and had grown close to many of the local athletes who now shunned him and the league.

"It was a hard struggle for me because I was friends with a lot of the former players from the late '50s," Mycock said. "Even though they were phased out gradually, it was still tough on many friendships."

CAPE BASEBALL SNAPSHOTS
Lights out in Chatham during the 1971 All-Star Game

One of the more memorable dates in Veterans Field history as well as league history occurred in 1971, when Chatham hosted an All-Star Game between the CCBL and the Atlantic Collegiate Baseball League. It was just the second All-Star tilt between the two leagues, with the first matchup taking place at Yankee Stadium and the CCBL coming out on the good end of a 6–3 score. The Cape League wanted to present a beautiful spectacle for amateur baseball fans everywhere.

The newly refurbished park had just had a new light system installed (finished a year behind schedule) that had cost $41,000, and there was a capacity crowd on hand. The stands behind home plate were full, and lawn chairs had been spread down the right and left field lines. A large crowd was also sitting on the right field bluff beyond the fence.

The pre-game ceremonies were full of pomp and circumstance. Newscaster Jack Hynes was the master of ceremonies, introducing former Red Sox great Joe Cronin, Hall of Famer Frankie Frisch, league commissioner Bernie Kilroy, H. Kline Weir (who had donated the lights), and a representative from the governor's office.

Despite a summerlong draught, the Chatham groundskeepers had worked overtime to ensure that the playing field was a deep green. The new lights had been tested and were in great shape. In the distance, the spires of Chatham caught the last rays of sunlight as the sun dipped below the horizon. All in all, a great evening for baseball.

And the Cape Leaguers were doing their part through the first three innings. In the top of the fourth, the CCBL held a 2–0 advantage. Bob Grossman of Orleans came in to relieve Falmouth's Paul Mitchell.

Grossman struck out the first two batters, and then . . . the brand new lights went out.

What to do? It was not quite dark yet, but it would be impossible to play baseball at this time of the evening without the use of the lights. Small boys ran onto the field and cavorted in what was called in one report an "eerie semidarkness." The players stood in front of their dugouts, waiting for some word from the league office.

What happened was that a blackout had not only knocked out the power in Chatham, but all across the Cape. Many threw their hands in the air in disgust and went home. Others who had lived through Cape Cod power outages many times before simply sat and wondered how long it would take for the electric company to patch things up.

After about 25 minutes, the lights came back on to a loud cheer. The Cape League continued their assault on the ACBL pitchers, scoring three more runs in the bottom of the fourth to take a 5–0 lead. But three runs from the ACBL in the top of the fifth cut the lead. Russ Peach of Falmouth came on in the top of the sixth to throw for the CCBL.

About that time, the field lights went out gain. But this time, it was for only another minute-and-a-half, and they returned at full-strength. "Everybody cheered. Nobody left the park," said the *Cape Codder.* The Cape League added a sixth run in the bottom of the seventh to finish the scoring, giving themselves a 6–3 win and a measure of respect in the growing rivalry between the two summer leagues.

As the league moved into the modern era with the election of a commissioner and the merger of the Upper Cape and Lower Cape divisions, the league began to draw more notice around the baseball world. The Red Sox pledged their support to Chatham for the year, supplying equipment in the form of old uniforms. "I think every uniform they sent was Walt Dropo's," Chatham's Tom Desmond recalls telling Merrill Doane at the time. Dropo was a huge man at 6'5" and 220 pounds; he filled out a uniform better than most. Other major league teams promised assistance in varying amounts.

In 1969, the Cape League consolidated their two divisions into one eight-team circuit, which would last only three years. In 1972, the league suffered its first real setback of the modern era when the Bourne Canalmen folded. But three years later, the league expanded again. The CCBL voted to place a team in Hyannis. The Hyannis Mets began play in 1976, bringing the number of teams back to eight. That same year, another summer college league began play. The Jayhawk League, based in Halstead, Kansas, quickly surpassed its midwestern counterparts as the place to play. During this time, many of these other successful summer collegiate leagues that began in the '60s began to hit their stride. While the CCBL joined summer college leagues in Alaska, Illinois, Virginia, and New Jersey that were known for their talent, the Cape League still served as the standard according to former league president Mike Curran.

"I remember attending a meeting at the NCAA convention in Washington, D.C. in the early '70s," Curran told the *Cape Cod Times* in 1976. "Those conventions were our only contact with the other summer leagues. And when we walked in, these people from the other leagues knew who we were, and they sensed we were the top competition."

In addition to the added respect that the Cape League had garnered throughout the '70s, it was also gaining respect throughout professional baseball. The first wave of modern, prestigious alumni began to make an impact at the major league level. Players who toiled on the Cape League diamonds in the late '60s and early '70s, such as Carlton Fisk, Thurman Munson, Tom Grieve, Charlie Hough, Mike Flanagan, and Steve Stone were all gaining attention in the majors in the mid- to late-'70s.

And it wasn't only the players who were making a name for themselves. Several of the Cape League umpires received sudden promotions twice in the 1970s when the major league umpires went on strike. Curly Clement remembers the phone call he got from Boston Red Sox owner and general manager Haywood Sullivan one afternoon while he was working at King's Department Store.

"This is Haywood Sullivan," said the voice on the other end of the line.

"Haywood who?" Clement responded.

Cotuit manager Jim Hubbard (left) and Red Sox manager
Johnny Pesky (second from left) compare notes with
Kettleers Joe Russo and Connie Deneault at Fenway
Park in 1963. The major leagues have always
supported the Cape League in one form or
another, either financially or otherwise.
Photo courtesy of Arnold Mycock.

"Haywood Sullivan, the general manager of the Boston Red Sox," he replied. "We want you to umpire tonight. The umpires are out on strike."

"Who are you kiddin'?" Clement asked. Clement knew Sullivan's son, Marc, who played for Orleans, and would go on to play for the Red Sox.

"No, Curly," Sullivan said. "I've got to call some other guys. I'll call you back."

Clement ended his conversation with Sullivan and called his wife Adrienne.

"Did you see on TV that the umpires are out on strike?" Clement asked his wife.

"No," his wife answered. Clement thought nothing more of it until his friend and fellow umpire Bob Giard called later that afternoon. Then, he spoke with Sullivan again.

"Haywood, how did you get my name?" Clement asked.

"You've been highly recommended by the scouts and my son," Sullivan responded. "We want you here."

Clement ended up working the game between the Angels and the Red Sox. The game went by without incident, with Clement working third base. But the major leagues received an injunction, and Curly's major league season came to an unceremonious end.

"We were supposed to work Friday, Saturday and Sunday," Clement said. "I had the plate for Sunday. But the judge put in an injunction on their strike, and made the umpires go back to work on Saturday. So when we went to umpire the game on Saturday afternoon, all our gear and luggage was in the basement. They threw it all out. Nice guys, huh?"

"I think the league had a great growth spurt in the 1970s," said Dick Sullivan, who served as both president and commissioner at the time. "I'm proud of it. We accepted the Hyannis Mets into the league. We had lots of our alumni become successful in professional baseball, at the major leagues, at that time. We were getting more and more high draft choices, and CCBL names were beginning to emerge on major league rosters as well. We started getting who would become Rookie's of the Year, MVP's and Cy Youngs and such, an extraordinarily impressive list. And the fan base continued to build."

The sudden growth of the league on the national level in the mid-80s contrasted sharply with the low-level growth that occurred in the mid-70s. While the league leaders of the 1970s were more concerned with simply getting the word out about the talented players that were taking part in the CCBL, in the 1980s, they began measuring themselves against the rest of the baseball world.

Dick Sullivan served as the commissioner of the league from 1975 through 1978, and returned to serve as president from 1984 through 1986.

"We grew during that (first) period," Sullivan told the *Cape Cod Times* in a 1987 interview. "We tried to bridge the gap between the old town team league and the college league. It was pivotal in going from a collegiate league that was good to one that was the best in the country."

At this time, the league managed to win back many of the local media outlets that had shunned them in the ´60s when local players were on their way out. As a result, daily coverage of league activities began to turn up more and more in Cape media outlets. And as more and more former Cape Leaguers made the major leagues, the CCBL also began to find their way into the national spotlight. In 1981, they found a way to fill the void that was created by the major league baseball strike. That year, the league received national attention during the players' strike when publications such as the *New York Times* and *Sports Illustrated* paid the Cape League a visit. A photo essay and full-page story entitled "A Parade of Young Pearls" by *SI* baseball writer Steve Wulf gave Cape Cod a chance at the national sports spotlight.

It was all part of a master plan to manipulate the media, according to former league commissioner and president Dick Sullivan.

"We felt it was important to let people know about this league, and we became actively involved with media people to let them tell the story," Sullivan told the *Cape Cod Times* in 1987. "We wanted to be the very best league in the country, and collectively, we decided to do everything first class."

And it didn't stop with the 1981 articles in *Sports Illustrated* and the *New York Times*. They cultivated a relationship with local cable network ESPN (with the hope of possibly exploring a television contract, according to many sources — something that never happened) and were profiled in *USA Today*.

The year 1984 again gave the league a chance to flex its collective muscles. It hosted a contest between the league all-stars and a team of United States Olympians. Players such as Will Clark, Cory Snyder, Charles Nagy, and others who were Cape League alumni returned to Cape Cod for a game at Chatham's Veterans Field. Olympian Oddibe McDowell provided the highlight, smashing a home run off of the fire station beyond the right field hill.

As attendance swelled and television ratings soared, baseball enjoyed a renaissance at the major league level in the mid-80s. The Cape League prepared to go along for the ride, as the second crop of modern-day CCBL alumni were starting to make their mark at the major league level. Older players such as Fisk and Hough were followed by several up-and-coming notables. The name "Cape League" was starting to take on a luster throughout the world of organized baseball.

A week or so before the 1985 season was scheduled to begin, major league baseball's annual amateur draft was held. It was perhaps the CCBL's finest hour of the post-1963 era. Six former Cape Leaguers were selected in the first round, including Will Clark (second overall to the Giants) and Canton native Bobby Witt (third overall by the Rangers), followed by Pete Incaviglia (eighth to the Expos), Walt Weiss (11th to the Athletics), Joe Magrane (18th to the Cardinals) and Joey Cora (23rd to the Padres). The six Cape Leaguers in the first round tied a record for most players drafted from a summer college league.

A possible seventh, B.J. Surhoff, was taken first overall by the Milwaukee Brewers. However, Surhoff's Cape League claims are disputed; while he was on the 1983 Wareham roster, he spent the summer with the U.S. Pan Am team. In addition, three Cape Leaguers were taken in the first round of the draft's secondary phase, which includes players who had been drafted previously.

More than ten years later, many still consider it the finest ama-

Several national media outlets descended on Cape Cod in the late '80s. This cover story on the CCBL (featuring Y-D pitcher Dennis Neagle) appeared in the July, 1989 issue of *M Magazine*. Photo courtesy of Don Tullie.

teur draft that the major leagues has ever had. In addition to Surhoff, Clark, Witt, Incaviglia, Weiss, Magrane, and Cora all having extensive careers in the majors, 1985 saw such future superstars drafted as Barry Larkin, Barry Bonds, Rafael Palmeiro, Randy Johnson and David Justice, all within the first four rounds.

Many reports had Clark ready for the bigs immediately. However, Giants executive vice-president Tom Haller said that "he needs to get acclimated to the wood bat. The major leagues is a different animal."

As the season opened, Haller's words were eerily prophetic. The league was set to return to wooden bats for the first time since the 1960s. The Cape Cod Baseball League has used wooden bats since its inception in 1923, but had switched over to the cheaper aluminum ones in the '60s. But the change disenchanted professional scouts, as well as baseball purists.

The reintroduction of wooden bats was a bold move. It would put the CCBL light years ahead of other leagues in the eyes of professional scouts. This way, scouts could truly gauge a hitter's ability at a high level. It would be several years before another summer college league would make the switch to wooden bats.

"Money was a big issue," league president Judy Scarafile told the *Cape Cod Times* when reflecting on the decision a few years later. "Who was going to pay for it? But the fans loved it and it really set us apart. The wooden bats brought back true baseball."

"We're going back to real baseball," trumpeted CCBL Commissioner Fred Ebbett in a June 9, 1985 interview with the *Cape Cod Times*. "Now, defense and pitching are important again. There was too much offense with aluminium, there has to be a blend of all three."

According to Ebbett in that same interview, the idea began at the Association of Baseball Coaches of America (ABCA) at the Dallas, Texas convention the previous year.

"I brought the idea up at breakfast, sitting around with Judy Scarafile, George Greer, Larry Gallo and a few other coaches. George started to talk about how he liked the other idea, and the others started piping in too. That was the starting point. After coming back from Dallas we did a survey of players who were in

Will Clark (top row, second from left) was just one of six former Cape Leaguers taken in the first round of major league baseball's 1985 amateur draft. Clark, who was part of Cotuit's 1983 championship squad, was taken second overall by the San Francisco Giants.
Other Cape League alumni taken in the first round that year were Bobby Witt, Pete Incaviglia, Walt Weiss, Joe Magrane and Joey Cora. Photo courtesy of Arnold Mycock.

the league last year and coaches from across the country. Of the 200 responses, 156 were in favor of wooden bats. We approached the league executive committee, who said they would approve it as long as the majors would accept it."

"The move to wood back in '85 was huge," says *Boston Globe* and ESPN baseball correspondent Peter Gammons. "It took it to a place where guys could really prove they could really play. It also made things much easier for scouts, to gauge a hitter's ability."

The move helped players' prospects on two fronts. First, when they did well, their stock increased in the eyes of the scouts. Second, it made for a much more gradual adjustment to the unexpected rigors of hitting with wood bats once they arrived in the minors.

"It was probably the best step they could have made at the time to assert themselves as the preeminent league in the country," said Red Sox GM Dan Duquette, who was working with the Milwaukee Brewers at the time and remembers the announcement. "The kids became serious about developing their skills for a pro career, and the teams that are scouting the league for talent became serious, and those two things came together."

"As a collegian, you always have a certain curiosity as to how you would play with a wood bat, but you never know," said New York Yankees first baseman Tino Martinez, who played for Falmouth in 1986. "Everybody talks about what an adjustment it was. It gave me the opportunity to go out and play with a wood bat after my freshman year, so I knew after I got drafted I would be able to hit with it. It was just a matter of time getting used to it."

New York Mets infielder Craig Paquette takes the idea one step further.

"[Using the wood bat] has a lot to do with the confidence factor," said Paquette, who played for Brewster in 1988. "Like anything in pro ball, you need to establish confidence. The confidence factor after signing a professional contract, knowing I could use a wood bat, made the transition to the minors much easier."

But Toronto's Ed Sprague feels the transition to wood is easier because usually the entire team is going through the same process.

"It's kind of a fun transition, because everybody is making the jump at the same time," Sprague said. "It's not like pro ball where some guys have been doing it longer than others. Everybody is going through the same sort of thing, and you could work on some things with your teammates, talk about the same sort of thing."

"Anytime you use the wood bats for the first time, there is going to be an adjustment period," said Detroit Tigers infielder Bob Hamelin, who played for Harwich in 1987. "And I think it's a lot like the first time you get called up to the big leagues. It takes a while to feel comfortable, and it's the same thing with the wood bats. But the more experience (with the wood bats) that you get with them is going to help you."

Wood bats provided Chuck Knoblauch with his favorite Cape League moment.

"Other than winning the whole thing, my favorite moment from that summer was hitting my first home run with the wood bat," said Knoblauch, who played for Wareham in 1988. "It was in Harwich, I remember. It was pretty exciting. There were a lot of great moments, but winning it and hitting my first one with a wood bat, those were the best. It was real exciting."

The decision was officially ratified in January of 1985 at the ABCA Convention in Nashville. The major leagues increased their grant from $50,000 to $60,000 a year, and that was all it took. The CCBL gained for itself a level of respect unmatched throughout the college baseball world.

In addition, the league celebrated its 100th anniversary with an old-timers game held at Eldredge Park in Orleans.

The league's actual inception has always been a point of contention. The league has promoted 1885 as the true start of the Cape Cod Baseball League, despite evidence that indicates otherwise.

David Q. Voigt, writing in the December 1970 issue of the *New England Quarterly* about the history of the Boston Red Stockings, commented sharply on the number of seemingly fictional baseball centennials. "Celebrated . . . often with questionable historical accuracy, they function as rites of intensification for restoring baseball's longevity and virility. To the historian of sports with a trained suspicion of myth, such celebrations are a challenge to set the record straight."

But in 1985, the league decided to go ahead with an old-timers contest anyway. That matchup pitted former Lower Cape stars against some of the best players that the Upper Cape had to offer. There were players dating back to 1907, with 94-year-old Llewellen "Tod" Owen the oldest player on hand. Owen played second base for Falmouth in the ΄20s, but decided to sit out the game. Owen still felt strong enough to congratulate the league on its decision to return to the wooden bats earlier in the year.

"The aluminium bats make for cheap home runs," Owen said. "I didn't think that it was sporting, so I'm glad they went back to the wooden bats."

The honor of the oldest player in competition fell to 78-year-old Merrill Doane, who enjoyed a long and successful career with Chatham. He started on the 1923 squad, but could only manage a ground out in his only at-bat.

The stars of the game were the pitchers, among them Fred Thatcher and Noel Kinski (of the Upper Cape) and Glenn Rose, Bob Gill, and Tom Yankus (of the Lower Cape). In addition, other notable ballplayers showed up. The Cleary brothers, Bob and Bill played (the latter would go on to coach the Harvard hockey team to a National Championship in 1989). Bill was the victim of the game's prettiest play, an around-the-horn double play that brought the crowd to its feet. The Lower Cape ended up taking the contest, 2–1, but nobody on the Upper Cape squad seemed to mind.

The 1988 season can be called a watershed year for two reasons: league expansion and the arrival of the most talented group of players in nearly a decade.

The drama surrounding the 1988 season actually began the previous November at the annual league meetings in Harwich. The topic of expansion had been discussed throughout the mid-΄80s, and many decided that it was about time to expand the circuit. Attendance was booming, the league's popularity was at its peak, and other towns wanted in.

What many had assumed to be a quiet meeting regarding expansion began instead with a heated discussion about who would be the new president for the upcoming year, since league president Chuck Smith had decided to resign his post. Smith had a contentious presidency; he had clashed with then vice-president Judy Scarafile on a number of issues, including the idea of a proposed league all-star game instead of the CCBL's annual contest with the Atlantic Collegiate Baseball League. It was also reported that he thought the league should save money by going back to aluminium bats.

Smith had threatened to resign the previous month, only to be talked out of it. But this time he was serious, and it was left to the 36 league officers to bicker over a replacement. They settled on Scarafile.

Scarafile had risen through the ranks since she was first associated with the league as a scorekeeper in the summer of 1970. After graduation and marriage, she moved to the Cape and began working with the league on a full-time basis. She had served the league in various capacities, including director of public relations, deputy commissioner, and vice-president.

Scarafile would serve as interim commissioner until May 1988, when the position was assumed by former GM Dave Mullholland. She served as vice president until October of 1991, when she was elected league president.

After much rancor over the presidency, the topic of expansion was discussed, with Bourne, Brewster, Plymouth, Mashpee, and Sandwich as the five candidates. The league initially favored Sandwich, as they held a distinct historical advantage. Jack Aylmer remembers:

"When we proposed putting the Bourne team on the field, one of the objections was that it won't do much good going from eight to nine teams. So we were not going to vote the Bourne team in unless there was a 10th team.

"So we immediately looked at Plymouth, Sandwich and Mashpee to see if there was an appetite to field a team in any one of those towns. We looked at Sandwich and Mashpee particularly because there were historically ball-teams that did exist there, more so in Sandwich. I think Sandwich was one of the oldest communities to field a team in the Cape League. But Brewster had such a good proposal, we couldn't turn them down."

After a heated discussion it was decided to put the issue to a vote. By a 31–2 count, with three abstentions, they approved Bourne and Brewster as the newest members of the league.

The league now had its present 10-team format, including the Bourne Braves and the Brewster Whitecaps. Bourne would join the Cotuit Kettleers, Falmouth Commodores, Hyannis Mets, and Wareham Gatemen in the newly-formed Western Division, while Brewster would be in the Eastern Division with the Orleans Cardinals, Harwich Mariners, Chatham Athletics, and Yarmouth-Dennis Red Sox.

It would be the first time since the sixties that the league would be split up in two divisions. To that end, a new playoff system was devised. The top two teams in each division would face each other in a best-of-three playoff series, and the two winners would then face each other in another best-of-three championship round.

If the first wave of talented ballplayers in the modern era arrived at the major league level in the early '70s with Carlton Fisk, Thurman Munson, and Charlie Hough, and the second wave in the early '80s with players such as Mike Pagliarulo and John Tudor, the most talented class that would graduate to the big show arrived on the Cape in 1988. While college stars such as Brian Barnes, Kevin Morton, J.T. Bruett, Sam Drake, and Scott Erwin were some of the league's top players, it was the lesser known players (at that time) such as Frank Thomas, J.T. Snow, Jeff Bagwell, Mo Vaughn, Albert Belle, Tim Salmon, and Chuck Knoblauch who played on the Cape that summer, who would go on to successful careers in the majors.

That year also saw the league marketing a line of baseball cards. The 30-card set, produced by Ballpark Cards, featured such league favorites as Mo Vaughn, Frank Thomas, Jeff Bagwell and Chuck Knoblauch. Tim Salmon and Jeromy Burnitz were featured on team cards. In addition, P&L Promotions produced an 186-card set. It was this set that caught the attention and provoked the ire of the NCAA, which objected to the alleged unauthorized use of "NCAA" on the card fronts. The legal wrangling that followed prompted the league to decide that issuing future sets simply wasn't worth the hassle. As a result, the 1988 card sets have tripled in value, with many Cape card shops currently putting the value of both sets close to $90 each.

In addition, the start of the 1988 season saw an agreement with Major League Baseball to start an umpire development program with the CCBL. Set up much like the current system for players, it allowed promising young umpires who had just graduated from umpiring school to be placed with boarders on the Cape. They would work during the day to pay rent, and they would work as the third umpire in league games at night. They were not paid for their on-field work, but used the opportunity to showcase their talents and improve their chances for a trip to the majors.

Unfortunately, the program worked too well. Many of the best young umpires who enrolled in the program were called to the minor leagues in midseason, leaving the Cape League with a dearth of talented men in blue. The system was scrapped in 1991. But by that time, the league's reputation had been built up to the point that it had no trouble attracting top-flight umpires.

Former Speaker of the House and rabid baseball fan Thomas P. "Tip" O'Neill got the 1988 season started in Harwich by throwing out the first ball. Predictably, the league numbers for offense boomed that summer, even with most players using wooden bats for the first time at such a high level of play. Thomas (called "Franklin Thomas" in several stories over the year in the *Cape Codder*) hit five home runs (including three in one game) for Orleans, while Vaughn and Knoblauch (who played shortstop at that juncture) played for Wareham, and formed a portion of what might have been the best infield in Cape League history.

As the season rolled on, it became quite clear that the Wareham Gatemen were the class of the league. It also became clear that Vaughn and Knoblauch were two of the primary reasons why. Former Wareham GM John Claffey recalled Knoblauch:

"When you're asked about ballplayers," Claffey said. "If you're trying to be positive, you'll say, 'This guy is a great ballplayer' or 'This guy is a winner.' I've heard that about a lot of players, and it is a term that is overused, and hacked to death. But if there is one ballplayer that I've seen in my entire life in the game of baseball that is a winner, it is Chuck Knoblauch. I will put that in capital

CAPE COD PROSPECTS
FRANK THOMAS - 1B
ORLEANS CARDINALS

CAPE COD PROSPECTS
JEFF BAGWELL - 3B
CHATHAM A's

While with the Orleans Cardinals in 1988, Frank Thomas won
the home run hitting contest at the league all-star game, but
left town early because of football practice at Auburn.
That left a bad taste in the mouth of many Cardinals fans.

Both Chuck Knoblauch and Mo Vaughn formed the
cornerstone of the 1988 Wareham Gatemen, one of
the most successful teams in league history.
Cards courtesy of Arnold Mycock.

CAPE COD PROSPECTS
MAURICE VAUGHN - 1B
WAREHAM GATEMEN

CAPE COD PROSPECTS
CHUCK KNOBLAUCH - SS
WAREHAM GATEMEN

letters: That kid knew how to win games. I will never use that term again with any player I've been associated with. There are guys who are talented athletes, who give tremendous individual performances, but there's never been a guy who knows how to win a game like Chuck Knoblauch.

"I remember him standing on deck, waiting for his turn at bat. I always studied Knoblauch in a tight situation. He was so anxious to get in there, so focused on what the pitcher was doing, and so intense, he would start to sweat and have the veins pop out on his forehead. Through the entire season with Wareham, that guy produced every single game."

The other player who stood out from the 1988 team in Claffey's mind was Mo Vaughn, who put in a brief appearance the year before. Early in 1987, Vaughn had just left the Shenandoah League, because, by all accounts, he wasn't enjoying himself. But his mood changed the minute he stepped off the bus in Wareham.

"I'll never forget it," Claffey said of Vaughn's first appearance in 1987. "He came from Connecticut to Boston to the Cape on a Greyhound Bus. I went down to meet him at the bus terminal in Wareham. It was a priceless sight. Mo gets off the bus, and he's looking around. He sees me, and starts waving at me, smiling like a young kid, full of vim and vigor. He was like a kid, ready to go. We got him into a house, a good living arrangement, and he started to play for the Wareham Gatemen."

And that started a partnership that would last for the better part of two summers. Vaughn did everything that was asked of him, and more. That included catching both ends of a double-header against Falmouth.

"One day, we had to go down and play Falmouth, and both of our catchers were hung up with injuries," Claffey recalls. "So I had asked Mo if he would catch that day. Without hesitation, he said yes. Now, he had never caught before in his life. It was a brutally hot Sunday afternoon and he had to catch a doubleheader. He went out there, behind the plate, and gave 100 percent for those two games and did a helluva job."

But when he returned in 1988, Vaughn knew that, while it was important to have a talented team to win in the Cape League, it is sometimes even more important to have team chemistry. The 1987 team was talented, but had fallen apart due to some ill will among teammates, and Vaughn would make sure that it wouldn't happen again.

"He knew that we had had problems before," Claffey said. "In '88, he made damn well sure that it wasn't going to happen again. He was there early, in the dugout, on the field. 'C'mon, let's go, let's hustle, let's keep working.' A guy would start to slack off and Mo would be right on him."

Together, Vaughn and Knoblauch formed one of the most impressive infields in Cape League history. They also helped establish a winning tradition that still lives on in Wareham today.

"To have him and Mo on the same team was amazing," Claffey said. "We started as a great team with a lot of talent, but with injuries, by the end of the year, we were only a shell of the original team. But Mo and Chuck had established something that you just can't describe. They knew what they were going to do — they were going to play to win. And that is what they did."

The All-Star game was held at Eldredge Park in Orleans. The 5,000 fans who were on hand and those who arrived early got the chance to hear a jazz concert two hours before the game, and Red Sox legend Luis Tiant threw out the first pitch. But the highlight of the afternoon was the first annual homerun hitting contest. It might have been the greatest collection of talent in modern college baseball history, with eight future major leaguers among the 10 contestants. Hitting for the West were Mo Vaughn, Chuck Knoblauch, Mark Johnson, Jody Hurst and John Farrell, while the East countered with Frank Thomas, Jeff Bagwell, Eric Wedge, Dave Staton and Steve O'Donnell.

Despite a valiant attempt by the gritty Knoblauch, the home run contest came down to a battle between Frank Thomas and Brewster's Dave Staton, who was hotly pursuing the league's Triple Crown that year. By the end of the year, Staton would capture the league HR and RBI titles, but would miss out on the batting title by .002 to Knoblauch.

Using a black bat given to him by his Auburn football friend and future major league teammate Bo Jackson, Thomas hit four home runs in his first ten swings, a feat that was amazingly duplicated by Staton. The two attempted to end the tie break, but both hit one homer in five attempts.

Staton started the second tie breaker in the same fashion, going deep once in five swings. Thomas seemed to be heading toward another tie with Staton when he hit just one out of the park in his first three tries. But on the fourth, he lashed a long drive over the left field fence, and claimed the crown.

Baseball people were salivating at the talent that populated the league that year, but Thomas was primarily regarded as a football prospect.

"Not many people thought he was going to continue as a baseball player," said longtime league supporter Jeremy Gilmore. "In fact, he angered most of the fans at Orleans when he returned to Auburn for early football practice just about the time that the playoffs began. Of course, Orleans thinks Thomas's departure cost them the championship that year. I don't know whether they were right or wrong, but it did leave a bad taste in their mouth."

But the real display of talent would come at the end of the 1988 season, when the Cape League All-Stars traveled to Boardwalk and Baseball, a theme park that doubled as the Kansas City Royals spring training site in Florida, where they faced the best the other college summer circuits had to offer. The Shenandoah Valley League, the Great Lakes League, and the Central Illinois League all traveled to Florida for a tournament that is still remembered as one of the finest displays of amateur baseball in history. Wareham General Manager John Claffey recalls how the tournament was put together.

"It all started with a fellow by the name of Floyd Perry, who used to be a coach at several Florida junior colleges. When Baseball and Boardwalk opened up, he was named the manager of it. So we were at the college coaches' convention in January of that year, and he asked me about the idea of having a tournament down in Florida.

"I said 'Jeez, that would be great. Let me check with our league and our finances.' To make a long story short, the tournament was put together relatively quickly. The Great Lakes, the Central Illinois League, and the Shenandoah League all joined, and Floyd was the man that made it happen."

In the first contest that Friday night, the Cape League faced Great Lakes, and were tied at two entering the ninth inning. But a late error by Jeff Bagwell opened the floodgates for four runs, and Great Lakes won by a 6–2 count. Claffey says that this game, and that inning in particular, was a touchstone in Bagwell's career.

"Jeff Bagwell's problems, at the time, were his hands," Claffey remembers. "Down at Boardwalk and Baseball, we were playing on an artificial surface (an artificial turf infield and a grass outfield) and Jeff is struggling at third base, and he had a couple of tough plays.

"Then he booted the ball in the ninth and Stan Meek called time and went out to see the pitcher. Bagwell comes walking in from third base to join the conversation, and there were tears coming down his face. So the catcher, Eric Wedge, tried to pick him up, saying 'C'mon Jeff, take it easy. We're all struggling here, we're not doing too well. Don't worry about it.' But even after the game, when everyone was sitting together in the stands watching the game after ours, Jeff was sitting way off at the top of the bleachers, all by himself. I went up and said 'Hey Jeff, we're just here to have a good time. Don't worry about it.' So he started to relax, and things turned out all right. And he ended up doing pretty well in the tournament."

But after being saddled with the loss, the Cape Leaguers were faced with the tremendous feat of escaping the losers' bracket by winning their next four games if they wanted to have a shot at the title.

On Saturday, they eliminated Shenandoah with a 6–5 win. They also pounded Central Illinois, 11–1, setting up a championship matchup on Sunday with the Great Lakes League.

In the opener, the Cape League trailed 4–3 entering the bottom of the eighth inning. Jeff Bagwell had the inning's big hit, a double to left-center that knotted the game at four. Tim Salmon then singled him home with what proved to be the game's winning run. In a moment of irony, Salmon's game-winner came against Great Lakes lefty Eric Jacques, who had pitched for Yarmouth-Dennis the previous summer.

The Cape Leaguers went on to a 7–4 win, which forced a one-game, winner-take-all playoff to be played immediately.

Prior to the game, both teams agreed that it would be a seven-inning affair, as they both had to catch early evening flights.

Again, this contest was a come-from-behind affair for the Cape Codders, who faced a 1–0 deficit entering the top of the third inning.

But it was Salmon and Chuck Knoblauch (who would be named "Outstanding Pro Prospect" along with Most Valuable Player at the tournament) who got things started in the third. Salmon knocked a two-run homer, and Knoblauch added a run-scoring triple that would give the Cape a 6–1 edge.

Great Lakes struck back for three runs in the fifth, but when the Cape Leaguers scored twice in the top of the seventh to make the score 8–4, they mentally began to check their carry-on luggage for the flight home.

The lead was entrusted to Chatham's Michael LeBlanc, who was 5–0 with five saves for the Athletics that year. Despite being rocked for three runs in just one-third of an inning on Thursday, he had returned to the mound that Sunday afternoon, determined to redeem himself. But a walk to Great Lake's Terry Rupp was followed by three straight hits. With nobody out and the tying run on second, the score was suddenly 8–7.

But LeBlanc settled down, and retired the side on strikes. The Cape Leaguers breathed a sigh of relief and boarded the plane home with the honor of being the summer's best collegiate baseball league. The win was celebrated in the *Cape Codder* with the headline "Wood Still Makes The Biggest Noise As Cape League Stars Take Title." Claffey says that many of the friendships that were forged during the tournament were more important than the baseball that took place that weekend.

"We stayed at the Holiday Inn across the street from the ballpark," Claffey said. "Boardwalk and Baseball fed us two meals a day, we all ate together, and the kids were tremendous. There were a lot of friendships made, and you could see them forming. Many of them last to this day."

As major league salaries continued to skyrocket in the late '80s, many baseball fans became disgusted with the outrageous paychecks of the players and the equally outrageous antics of the owners. There was a wide-scale embrace of the minor leagues and college baseball. Fans yearned to get back to the grassroots level of the game, and the Cape League provided their fix.

The drama continued the next year. During the first week of June 1989, the Baltimore Orioles knew that they had the first selection in the upcoming amateur draft, and there was little doubt who they would select. Ben McDonald, a big, hard-throwing right-hander out of Louisiana State University, was considered the top prospect. The lanky, 6'7" right-hander had amazed professional scouts at the College World Series that year, and many believed he could make an immediate impact at the major league level. When he was selected number one, it shocked nobody, not even the Orleans Cardinals, who held McDonald's Cape League rights.

But as June gave way to July, it was clear that the negotiations weren't going to be as easy as many had originally anticipated. Rumors began to circulate. Would he sign with the Orioles? If so, when? Would he continue to hold out, and pitch in the Cape League?

Meanwhile, the Cardinals waited. They were in no hurry, but one thing began to distress them. Early in the year, they had been forced to make several roster moves, and now they were only allowed one more. Should they add McDonald to their roster, even if he didn't come, thus eliminating any other moves for the remainder of the season? And what if McDonald did show up, wanting to play, but Orleans was unable to add him to their roster?

It soon became clear that the negotiations were going to be long and drawn out. McDonald flew into Boston on July 17, and arrived in Bourne that night to see his new teammates drop a 5–0 decision to the Braves. With McDonald finally on the Cape, the Cardinal's coaching staff decided he would take his turn in the rotation three nights later when Orleans returned to Eldredge Park to face Harwich.

But the evening featured an overcast sky and a light rain, which gave the Cardinals cause for worry. What if they added McDonald officially to their roster, only to have the game rained out and have him sign the contract with Baltimore the next day? And rumors suddenly popped up that the Orioles and general manager Roland Hemond were going to call at any minute, agreeing to McDonald's demands for a $1 million signing bonus and a three-year, guaranteed salary.

As the 7 P.M. game time approached, McDonald hid in the Orleans clubhouse. He had been out of action since the second week of June, when the Louisiana State University Tigers had been eliminated from the College World Series, and was anxious to show the baseball world what he could do.

But the 4,000 fans, many of whom had been there since 4:30 that afternoon, continued to wait patiently, including the autograph hounds who stood five-deep behind the bullpen cage. The Cape League had played host to many stars in its day, but it had never seen the Number One pick in the country.

Satisfied that the rain would hold off, and still hearing nothing from the Orioles, Orleans manager John Castleberry made a decision. Five minutes before game time, he stuck his head out of the door of the Orleans clubhouse beyond right field and gave a thumbs-up sign to league commissioner Fred Ebbett, who was seated in the press box behind home plate. The nation's Number One draft pick was now officially an Orleans Cardinal.

McDonald pitched four innings against the Mariners. He threw 63 pitches, struck out three batters and allowed three walks and one hit.

"This was a good little workout," McDonald told the assembled media throng after the game. "That's the reason I came here. I didn't come to set records or win any championships. I came to get my arm in shape."

And that good little workout was McDonald's last on the Cape. Later that week, he flew back to Louisiana. Less than three months later, he was in the major leagues with the Baltimore Orioles, pitching in the midst of a pennant race against the Toronto Blue Jays.

McDonald was part of the third wave of modern-day alumni who hit the majors. Young stars like McDonald, Frank Thomas, Albert Belle, Chuck Knoblauch, Mo Vaughn, Tim Salmon and Jeff Kent all arrived in the majors in a two-year span, and players such as Jeff Bagwell, Bob Hamelin, and Charles Nagy would soon fol-low them. All made a major impact, winning MVPs and Rookie of the Year titles, along with a World Series championship.

· 7 ·

The Big Business ´90s

In the ´80s, the Cape League started to mean a lot more to base-ball fans because they started to get in touch with the grass roots aspects of baseball. It was one of the reasons that minor league baseball started doing well. I think as the big league baseball players and ballparks moved away from the fan, a certain section of fans started reaching back for something they could touch and be a part of, and the Cape Cod League afforded that.
—Steve Buckley of the *Boston Herald* and WEEI-AM

Starting with the untimely death of commissioner Bart Giamatti late in the 1989 season, major league baseball started down a path of discord and disrepair. From the earthquake that altered the ´89 World Series, through the owners' lockout at the start of the 1990 season, the unceremonious dumping of Commissioner Fay Vincent in 1992, and the players' strike of 1994, the major leagues seemed on the brink of ruin. It was only a matter of time before the shadow was cast over the Cape League. In the winter of 1994, the league learned that, along with the other summer college leagues, the annual $85,000 grant that had been awarded to the CCBL was cut because of the strike. The money had been coming in from the major leagues for many years, and the league had come to depend on the cash to get through the summer. But the Cape League wasn't the hardest hit. Funding for four of the 10 summer college leagues that Major League Baseball had supported in the past was to be cut drastically, according to an MLB spokesman. Funding was cut at other levels as well, including American Legion and Pony League baseball.

How had the Cape League gone about raising money in the years before the strike hit? Through five venues:

1. From the league towns. The towns usually supplied the league with sizable grants. This had not been a very popular move in the ´60s when teams began importing college players from around the country at the expense of the local talent. But when the towns and their fans came to realize how profitable a venture Cape League baseball could be, the money began to flow.

2. From Major League Baseball and the NCAA.

3. Through the advertising that teams sold in their game programs. Each club prints a game program with notes about each player and the college they come from, along with a brief history of the team and a list of thank you's to the volunteers who help keep the organization together.

4. Through the sale of souvenirs. Each team sells souvenir items like caps, t-shirts and pennants that always go over well with the sizable number of tourists that make up much of the crowd at an average Cape League contest. In addition, local restaurants and catering services often provide ballpark fare (ice cream, hot dogs, soda, etc.). From the "Bird's Nest" in Orleans to the Kettleers Kitchen in Cotuit, the souvenir/food stand is a major money maker for teams throughout the league.

5. By passing the hat at games. Often, a player or two not scheduled to take the field that night will join volunteers and wander through the crowd soliciting donations for the team. This, usually

combined with a nightly 50-50 raffle (where people buy lottery tickets, and the holder of the winning ticket gets half the pot, with the rest going to the team), is enough to push clubs into the black most years.

Financing the league has been a problem since the league's inception. A 1928 article in the *Barnstable Patriot* said that "altho the gate receipts were up to the usual average, the heavy expense of operating a team in the league makes financial support from other sources a necessity."

In 1933, after the Barnstable team ran into desperate financial straits, the *Patriot* published a detailed report of club costs. Into the third week of July, contributions from assorted groups (such as the Hyannis Board of Trade) and "concerned citizens" totaled $222. Total gate receipts came to $258.16. The expenditures, complete with arithmetical errors, were listed as follows:

Bleachers (maintenance and upkeep)	$30.00
Insurance (in case fans or players were injured)	$23.46
Stockings and caps	$16.50
Lumber for scoreboard	$ 1.33
Lime (for laying the first and third base lines)	$ .90
Scorebook (for official scorer, who would later report the score to the local papers)	$ .75
Hose for showers	$ 2.00
Total	$74.94

Baseballs	$ 44.10
Room and board	$171.10
Telephone and telegrams	$ 20.98
Transportation	$ 59.00
Ball chaser	$ 5.25
Advertising	$ 3.25
Cape Cod League (dues)	$ 15.00
Money paid to players	$111.00
Total expenditures	$494.79

Total receipts	$480.16
Total expenditures	$494.79
Deficit paid by manager Cook	$ 14.63

"Manager Cook lists the outstanding bills as follows

Printing	$ 22.50
signs	$ 30.75
room and board	$129.00
F.B. & F.P. Goss	$ 3.25
uniforms	$ 40.00
players salaries	$380.00
Total	$605.50

Manager Cook estimates the average weekly cost of running the team as $285." It was also revealed during the season that Cook had put some of the players up at his mother's house, and there were insufficient funds to help pay the bills, most notably the weekly food bills.

Various admission fees were charged at many of the ballparks throughout the 1930s, but supporters often took other fans to task for not doing their part to help their team. Many newspapers, including the *Enterprise* and the *Patriot*, would often chastise fans for failing to contribute, and ran totals of how much was collected at each contest each week during the 1934 season.

But sometimes the *Patriot* would go overboard. An August 22, 1935 story declared: "Barnstable fans fall way below Falmouth and Harwich in the way of supporting their teams through the collections. The collection at Osterville on Sunday was a little less than $40.00. Falmouth reported that it had received nearly $150 at the Heights on Sunday. The collections at the Harwich fields on Saturdays have been upwards of $100 whereas the games at Hallett's field are between $30 and $45. It would be easy to finance the team if every fan contributed 25 cents or somewhere near it at a game. The collectors wonder if folks are playing fair when they spend twice as much for peanuts and popcorn as they put into the hat?"

The situation was often the same in Falmouth. Five years before, an August 8, 1925 story in the *Enterprise* sounded the same reproachful tone: "The management of the Falmouth team are not exactly satisfied with the collections taken at the games at Falmouth Heights. The crowds in attendance would indicate that they would receive a much larger amount than is usually contributed. The team is running behind their expenses this season and if every patron would be as liberal as possible towards the support of the team, the team would be able to meet all expenses."

One supporter who was apparently cynical about Cape Cod baseball quickly changed his mind after a 1934 contest between Barnstable and Falmouth. The fan gave a dime to collectors in the fifth inning, but after a typically intense finish between the two rivals, "he hunted out the collector after the game and gave him $1 for the game he had seen." But the idea of passing the hat often wasn't enough to support teams in the '30s. The Barnstable teams staged "Tag Days," as well as an "Old Home Day" at Hallett's Field in 1936 that raised $400.

At the start of the 1937 season, the *Barnstable Patriot* lauded fans who came through the gates "without a murmur" and paid their admission without a problem. In the same article, they seemed to disdain the idea of passing the hat to raise funds: "Passing the hat is neither fun nor fair. No one likes the job. There is no reason why some people should pay a quarter and some people should pay a penny. One day, a man paid a penny for himself and his wife. The July 5th game will go down on the books as the occasion when the [Barnstable Athletic] association gained its independence of Hat Passing and the fans deserve credit for endorsing this new set-up." The story goes on to say that this new policy "gave the association the largest single game receipts since it has sponsored the Barnstable team."

It is believed that the return to passing the hat occurred in the late '50s and early '60s, when the league changed to an all-college circuit. During this time, the league began receiving cash from the NCAA and the major leagues.

The major leagues began contributing to the summer college leagues in 1971, with the amount steadily growing throughout the

1970s and 1980s. When the late '80s rolled around, the league was in good financial shape. In such good shape, in fact, that they began to talk about expansion. But the task of selling a town on the idea of having a Cape League franchise was not an easy one, recalls Jack Aylmer. Aylmer helped start the Hyannis and Bourne franchises. They may have been created 20 years apart, but the basis of their beginnings was the same. Aylmer knew how to sell the idea of a town on starting their own team.

"You sell them on economics, and you stress the virtues of baseball for toddlers," remembers Aylmer. "And you stress the advantages of being a host family. If you have a Babe Ruth or Little Leaguer in your household to start with, and you bring in a collegiate ballplayer, they'll be in seventh heaven. To this day, many of these relationships with host families continue to exist — the Christmas card if he is not so famous, the visit to Fenway Park if the player is lucky enough to make the major leagues."

In the winter of 1994, the league had saved $75,000 in what President Judy Scarafile called a "contingency fund," but was reluctant to use it. It was a safety net, and they didn't want to spend it all, only to be left with an empty cupboard if the league failed to receive any financial support from the major leagues the following year as well.

"We could use the entire fund to meet our expenses for next season, but what happens if we fall short in '96?" asked Scarafile. "If we need it, we use it, but we would like to be in a situation where we won't need that much of it. It's a nest egg we don't want to use all at once."

The 1994 players' strike that prompted this conservative approach wasn't the first time that the league had been threatened with the loss of the major league money. With the specter of a players' lockout looming at the start of the 1990 season, then-Cape League President John Claffey felt that it might be time then to cut the cord with the major leagues.

"It's been my feeling for a long time that the Cape League is too dependent on the grant," he told the *Cape Cod Times* in 1990. "This might be a hard lesson for us, but it could be a good one.

We're now looking at possible corporate sponsorship and more aggressive fund raising. We'll always need major league baseball's help, but we'd like to get ourselves in a position where we are a little more self-sufficient."

"But even though the money is already there, the question is whether or not major league baseball will release it," league commissioner Fred Ebbett said in the same story. "I think they will. I don't think they'll let us die."

Even today, years after his presidency, Claffey still feels the Cape League was headed down a road to ruin, depending far too much on a single source for the majority of their income.

"The amount of money that [major league baseball] gave us in 1990 was around $75,000 a year," he remembers. "That was 75 percent of our budget at the time. With the exception of Coca-Cola, who gave us $10,000 at the time, and Bradlees, which made a small donation as well, we had to find different sources of income. It's best to have 10 people contributing $10,000 than one donating $100,000, because if one guy falls by the wayside, you can always find someone else to pick up the slack. But if one guy is giving you $100,000 falls by the wayside, you've got a hell of a big job on your hands."

In 1994, Claffey's idea of a Cape League not dependent on the major league grant was about to happen. But in what seemed like its darkest hour, the Cape League rallied. A "Preserve the Tradition" fund drive was started, and the league began seeking funds from individual and corporate sponsors and donors. They talked about getting a local television contract with SportsChannel (an idea that never came to fruition). They applied for grants from various baseball and non-baseball related foundations, and became more aggressive when it came to collecting money at ballgames.

"We really don't know why MLB reduced the grant, and, to tell you the truth, it's really not that important," Scarafile said. "Maybe it's because we have better fund-raising abilities in place."

George Pfister, supervisor of baseball operations for Major League Baseball in 1995, said that they made the cuts reluctantly.

"This is the first time we've had to cut support," he said in a February, 1995 interview with the *Boston Globe*. "When baseball was prosperous, there were increases almost every year. But the income isn't there. We have to face reality."

That same year, the Yawkey Foundation and Bank of Boston each donated $25,000, and Ocean Spray also made a contribution. In addition, the league signed an exclusive contract with Louisville Slugger to help defray the cost of wooden bats.

The exclusivity with Louisville Slugger also ended a local relationship between the CCBL and the Barnstable Bat Company. Under the terms of the agreement with Louisville Slugger, Centerville-based Barnstable Bat would not be allowed to provide its bats to any league players. Owner Tom Bednark was upset.

"I don't understand it at all," Bednark told the *Barnstable Patriot*. "I'm sort of shocked. I had gotten a great response from players last season who used my bats (Jon Petke, the 1994 Cape League batting champion, used a BBC bat), and I was looking forward to having more players using my product."

"We are caught in a squeeze," Scarafile told the *Patriot* in the same story. "I would like to have that local flavor, but it was a choice I had to make. A choice that I was hoping I wouldn't have to make."

But most felt that Scarafile continued to do a tremendous job guiding the league through a difficult time.

"She's done a great job," said Dick Bresciani, who brought Scarafile into the league in the ´60s to assist with the public relations effort. Bresciani worked with the league in the late ´60s and early ´70s before taking a public relations job with the Boston Red Sox in 1972.

"Major league baseball had to cut back—they were still very generous to the Cape League, and have been—but Judy didn't just sit there and complain. She went out and looked for alternative ways, knowing that it took money to run the Cape League, to get money."

"I don't know if the league would have shut down, but it would have been a tough blow that would have almost killed it, if Judy didn't come through with the money," said Russ Charpentier, who covers the league for the *Cape Cod Times*. "The league was lucky that they had someone that smart. She just did a phenomenal job.

I mean, we've had our differences, but she sure gained my respect pulling the league out like she did."

Scarafile wanted to make sure that the individual teams remained financially solvent because it was imperative that the league not lose an individual team.

"We want to work together as a cohesive unit and not put a burden on the teams to raise funds for the league," Scarafile said. "Any money they raise will be for them."

When Scarafile referred to a cohesive unit, she was referring to the 10 teams that made up the Cape Cod Baseball League. But she could have just as easily been referring to the Cape itself. Businesses pitched in with financial help, as well as the promise of summer jobs for ballplayers. People sent checks of $10 and $25 to the league, hoping and praying that the league would remain solvent enough to struggle through another campaign.

And many believed that it was time that the towns begin to give more to the league. There was already in hand the monies pledged to the team by the town every year, but the league often gave back to the Cape much more in the form of tourist dollars.

The *Cape Cod Times* printed an editorial in January of 1995 titled "Preserve the Tradition" that called on people throughout the Cape to help pitch in and save the CCBL.

"The Cape Cod Baseball League has been part of the local landscape, in one form or another, for at least 109 years . . . The league is one of our staples of summer, right alongside sand dunes, seashells and seafood. But support from major league baseball is eroding and the Cape League will soon be asking its fans and neighbors for support through a 'Preserve the Tradition' fundraising campaign . . . The Cape Cod Baseball League contributes much to our community. When its representatives come calling with their pitch, step up to the plate and be a part of the action. They need and deserve everyone's help to preserve this truly great tradition."

One on-field tradition that ended in 1994 was the involvement of umpire Curly Clement, who was not asked back after 33 seasons as a Cape League umpire. Along the way, Curly survived four heart attacks, including two in the middle of Cape League games, (in 1982 and 1988), as well as a triple-bypass operation.

"They said that I couldn't do the job because I was getting too old, so they did not rehire me for the 1995 season," he said. "In 1994, I worked—between college, high school, the Cranberry League and the Cape League—89 ballgames. In 1995, between college, high school, Cranberry League, American Legion, Senior Babe Ruth and Yawkey League playoffs, I worked 141 games. Does that sound like a man that's too old?"

Known in baseball circles as "The Candy Man," he began handing out candy in the early '80s when he became sick and tired of watching players chew tobacco.

"I started with the candy in 1982," he recalls. "I used to buy it at Hickory Farms, and I used to buy anywhere between 25 to 45 pounds of candy every spring. I would start loading up in February or March. I was sick and tired of watching the guys chew tobacco. So I used to give them candy. Now, I see kids that I had in high school who are now playing American Legion, and they tell their kids to come up to me and ask, 'Hey Curly. Where's my candy?'"

By the 1996 season, the league had returned to fairly steady financial ground. So steady, in fact, that many league insiders scoffed at the idea that the Cape League was truly "amateur baseball."

"Unfortunately, we have become big business," said league officer Don Tullie in the summer of 1996. "It's a term I hate to use, but we're no longer just amateur baseball as we really think of amateur baseball. When you have franchises spending anywhere from thirty to ninety to one hundred thousand dollars a year, where the hell does amateur baseball fall into that?"

Many feel that the league is at a financial crossroads as it approaches the late 1990s.

"The league can't keep going the way it's going," Charpentier says. "When individual teams have to raise fifty to one-hundred thousand dollars, there's just too many people out there trying to raise money. Unfortunately, I think they're going to have to get a sugar daddy, a corporate sponsor that will have to foot the bill.

"How can Hyannis go out and raise $50,000? The league is going to have to remember that they're going to have to start helping out the franchises. Hyannis is going to have to find someone with money. Or the league is going to have to start helping them."

Many suggest that the Cape League executive committee members have to work together in order to help the league in the coming years.

"A Cape League meeting is unbelieveable," Charpentier says. "These people couldn't unite over a crosswalk. But they're going to have to unite for the good of the league."

"Each franchise has just one vote, and they are going to have to start realizing what's best for the league," said Tullie. "Not what's best for the Y-D Red Sox or the Bourne Braves. What's best for the league? What's going to keep this league intact? We have got to do that. It's very important."

Several people have talked about televising Cape League contests. There was talk during the winter of 1994 that the league was trying to get SportsChannel New England to put together a package that would include a "Cape League Game of the Week," but nothing came of it. Also, they have approached the New England Sports Network (NESN), carrier of the Boston Red Sox, Bruins, and many other college sports throughout New England. However, NESN has said that the cost of carrying these games would be too high.

"I think you might see the Cape League on television in the near future," says ESPN's Peter Gammons. "The problem is you have to have someone come in and explain to people the players you're looking for."

Radio has been tried sporadically, with little success or continuity. Radio broadcasts of Cape League games date back to the 1960s, when local teams tried to arrange it with town stations. According to many, stations like WCIB and WCOD have done the games in years past. But now, for the most part, broadcasts have been relegated to the all-star game. WKPE-AM broadcast some of the regular season games in 1994, but WCIB covered the 1994 midsummer classic, enlisting former Red Sox broadcaster Ken Coleman to bring the game to people throughout the Cape.

And as the Cape League continued to evolve off the field throughout the early '90s, things were changing on the field as well. Recruiting became a big business. Working in concert with their general managers, most Cape League field managers, who also work at Division I, II or III colleges around America, began scouting the country for the best available talent.

"Rolando Casanova (former manager at Orleans) and I worked closely together," says former Orleans GM Dave Mulholland, who put together the 1993 Orleans Cardinals team, which had collegiate superstars like Nomar Garciaparra and Jay Payton. "He knew a lot of people in the South, plus he'd built up relationships with coaches throughout the country.

"But the bottom line is Rolando had the final say on all kids."

That's usually the *modus operandi* throughout the league today, though many general managers will also have a hand in the scouting process as well. At the end of the season, the coaching staff will sit down with the general manager and see who they would like to go after for the next year.

"We sit down the day after the season ends and start making calls," said Y-D GM Jim Hagemeister.

Players cannot be signed before October 1st for the upcoming season. However, when you have that player's signature on the dotted line, it is only the first step in a long and worrisome process.

Teams must first anxiously await the major league draft, and hope that their top prospects are not enticed by the lure of big money. This has been difficult in recent years, with the promise of big money awaiting players who decide to sign on the bottom line.

It's a worry that has been with the league for several decades. A worst-case scenario happened to the Chatham A's in the early stages of the 1968 season. The team had four first-round picks on their opening day roster. Boston Red Sox Vice-President of Public Relations Dick Bresciani, who was doing PR work for the league at the time, remembers:

"Chatham manager Joe Lewis had four number-one draft picks out of that year's draft, which had been done the week before. Bobby Valentine was one of them. He was just out of high school, and was going to go to USC. Rick McKinney from Miami of Ohio was the number one pick at third base for the Chicago White Sox. John Curtis, out of Clemson, was a pitcher and the Red Sox number one draft pick. And Thurman Munson, from Kent State, was the number one pick for the Yankees, and he, like Curtis, had also

League president Judy Scarafile and longtime league supporter Don Tullie have kept the league financially solvent throughout the ´90s. Photo courtesy of Judy Scarafile.

Bobby Valentine (below), along with Thurman Munson, John Curtis and Rick McKinney were four first-round selections in the 1968 amateur draft who were slated to play for what was supposed to be a powerful Chatham A's that summer. However, all four of them signed before the season started, and Chatham finished with a 17–23 record.
Photo coutesy of Jack Aylmer

been at Chatham the year before. Joe was aware of what might happen. He said 'I'm sure I'm gonna lose *some* of them.' But they all signed contracts before the Cape League season opened and he lost every one of them."

Once the draft is done, the teams hope that no other summer college league grabs the player up, or that he doesn't opt to try out for Team USA, a national collegiate all-star team that plays an international schedule during non-Olympic years. However, many don't see the reasoning behind playing for Team USA, especially in a non-Olympic year.

"The summer of 1984, when I was in Orleans, was probably the best summer I ever had," said Blue Jays pitcher Erik Hanson. "As a matter of fact, I was contemplating going back and turning down the offer for Team USA in 1985."

"I'm a little curious as to why these guys get so hung up on playing for Team USA," says Peter Gammons, baseball writer for the *Boston Globe.* "They play with aluminum, they don't face consistent competition, and the whole thing about participating for your country . . . it's just not that big a deal. [The Cape League] is a much better league, and a much better place for a top prospect to play."

But it's not just Team USA that is in competition for the best collegiate players these days. As of the late 1990s, the number of summer college baseball leagues had grown to 17, with several more in the works. Stretching from metropolitan New York to Alaska to California to Kansas to Massachusetts, the college leagues provide a chance for the best college talent to improve their chances of making it to the major leagues. In addition, it helps scouts pinpoint some of the best college talent in a concentrated area. If a scout cannot see a prospect during the regular season — and many of the college baseball seasons last for two months or less, due to bad weather or bad teams — he can see how they fare in the high-intensity environment of a summer college baseball league.

In most of these leagues, the situation is the same as the Cape League: players are recruited from various college programs, they are coached mostly by college coaches, and they are promised the chance to work during the day and play baseball at night. And like the Cape League, they bring together a wide collection of base-ball talent, everyone from top-flight, Division One talent to that Division Three diamond-in-the-rough who often goes on to the major leagues.

All the leagues use wood bats, or Baum bats (a facsimile that looks and feels like wood, but doesn't break). All are NCAA sanc-tioned and receive the organization's financial backing. While most other leagues can point to a handful of former players in the ma-jors, the list of Cape League alumni with major league experience, as of 1993, was over one thousand, and continuing to grow.

Probably the strongest of the competition is the Alaskan Base-ball League. Based in Fairbanks, Alaska, they started play in 1964, and split into two leagues (the ABL and the Alaskan Central Base-ball League) in 1989. Players such as Tom Seaver, Dave Winfield, John Olerud, Frank Viola, and Jimmy Key have all spent their sum-mers in Alaska.

In addition, a select number of college players and coaches have split their time between Alaska and the Cape. Bill Mosiello has worked as a manager of the Brewster Whitecaps, and also spent time in Alaska with the Mat-Su Miners and the Anchorage Pilots. He feels that while the level of play on the field is about the same, the Cape holds a distinct advantage when it comes to the off-field activity.

"Where I was at Mat-Su, there is nothing to do," Mosiello said. "You can barely get something to eat. The weather is pretty good there, but it's nothing compared to Cape Cod."

Jamie Splittorf is another who has spent time in both the Alaskan and Cape Leagues. The son of former major leaguer Paul Splittorf, he says that Alaska is "probably the second best summer league," but agreed with Mosiello's opinion of off-field life, and added that things were definitely geared toward outdoors activities.

"Anchorage is like any other big city, and you can do any sort of big city things there," Splittorf said. "But I was in a small town, so if you liked fishing and hunting, that was the thing to do. I'm not really into that, so I didn't have much to do."

"I think that some of the long-term administrators from the different franchises on the Cape always try to figure out what's happening in Alaska," said Jack Aylmer, who has been associated with the Bourne, Cotuit, and Hyannis franchises. "Alaska is basically the only significant threat to talent for the Cape League."

As a result, the Cape League must battle the inducements that the Alaskan Leagues offer. According to Cape League sources, the ABL, at one time, offered things like "spring training" for two weeks in Hawaii, and tournaments in Japan, Colorado, and Southern California. In addition, players are flown to games because of the great distances between towns.

"You try to throw in something extra," said Aylmer, "because the Alaskan league is throwing in a round-trip three game series in Japan. The franchises are so far apart that you fly to games, and a job up there is sweeping out the press box. Here, the players have the drudgery of getting up early and going into a retail store and actually doing work. So you have to throw inducements into the mix."

Another aspect that draws the savvy ballplayer to the Cape instead of the Midwest is the fact that many people in the baseball establishment seem to prefer the warm summer breezes and the crack of real wood on Cape Cod. The wooden bats, as well as the proximity of the parks to one another make the Cape an ideal location for major league scouts. The longest distance between two parks is from Orleans to Wareham—a mere 46 miles. Many scouts take in two or three games in one day.

"I think the proximity of the parks makes it an attractive setting for scouts," says former Seattle Mariner scout Jack Webber. "Harwich and Brewster are just within a few miles of each other. The longest haul is no great shakes."

"From a scouting standpoint, it's nice that you can normally catch two games in one night, or at least parts of two games in one night," said Colorado Rockies scout Art Pontarelli. "So from that standpoint, it's pretty important. And also from the players' standpoint, it's a good thing because they don't have to travel all that far to get to ballgames."

"Alaska is just not as good a place to play," says Gammons. "Most scouts only make runs in and out of Alaska. It's just not the same. Gary Hughes (currently a major league scout with the Marlins who used to scout the area for the Expos) says he gets a condo in Orleans for two weeks every summer. It's that kind of exposure that sets the Cape apart. Don't get me wrong. Alaska is nice. And the Jayhawk League is very good. But this is the best place to play because the scouts all come here."

"History has shown that a number of the better ballplayers are going to be down here," Pontarelli said flatly. "It's considered to be one of the better college leagues for the summer, and with the environment that's down here, with the players, the coaching, it's the place to be for a scout."

But many major league insiders believe that nothing can match the experience.

"The summer college experience is great training for a ballplayer," said Red Sox GM Dan Duquette. "You get the best athletes and the best players in the U.S. into the summer leagues. It's a great league for travel, and the players also get a chance to see top-flight pitching. They have the additional benefits of being able to make the adjustment to the wooden bats. The hitters, as well as the pitchers."

"One thing it does for college kids is that it takes the college competition to another level," says former Texas GM Tom Grieve. "You just can't go to the Cape Cod League unless you're recommended as one of the top college players. So the players playing there are the guys that you would expect to be drafted in the first rounds of the draft.

"Also, now that they use wooden bats, it prepares the hitters and the pitchers for that next step, to get away from the aluminium bats, to see what the competition is like with a wooden bat."

"Former Twins GM Andy MacPhail said that both Chuck Knoblauch and David McCarty were both drafted out of the Cape League, and not off their college seasons," says Gammons.

Many players have compared their time in the Cape League to a minor league existence — playing an extended schedule without having to worry about classes, in addition to a two-month schedule for the first time away from home in small towns. Combined with living in towns that are just dots on the map the experience can prepare a professional prospect for the realities of minor league baseball. This will often cause a scout to recommend to his team to draft a certain player based not on his collegiate career, but his Cape League experience.

"You see a lot of prospects against some high-quality pitching," said Gammons. "You see them away from home, without college coaches. You see them out on their own, living almost a professional life."

Dick Bresciani has worked with the Boston Red Sox as Vice-President of Public Relations since 1972. Before that, he was PR Director of the Cape League for approximately five years. He has seen how the Cape League prepares a prospect for the majors.

"I think that [the Cape League] prepares them more for professional baseball than just for the major league level. Often, it's [player's] first time really being away from home on their own in a baseball- only situation, and they are overwhelmed.

"It's a 10-team league, and they have to travel. It's not great travel, the colleges today travel further distances, but [in the Cape League], you're not dealing with schoolwork and travel, you're dealing with just baseball. So I think it prepares you in that aspect, that when you get into the minor leagues, here you are with a bunch of guys you don't know, on a team in a highly competitive situation. Add to that the fact that you're going to be scouted at every single game."

However, the transition is tougher for West Coast natives who are making the trip east for the first time.

"It's really like playing in the minor leagues," said Tim Salmon of the Anaheim Angels. "I went all the way across the country for the first time and played in a small town. It was quite a bit different than Arizona, at least. It was a terrific experience, and gave me that little bit of fire for my final season in college to get ready for pro ball and what was to come."

"[Living away from home] was a big deal," says Boston Red Sox outfielder Damon Buford, who went to school at the University of Southern California. "If you're a young kid in college—I went to school right by my house, 20 minutes away—so that was really my first time getting out of the city and being almost entirely on my own—not entirely, there were always people looking

Three future first-round draft picks took part in the 1993 home run hitting contest over All-Star Weekend — Brewster's Brian Buchanan (back right, selected by the New York Yankees in 1994), Falmouth's Darin Erstad (front left, selected by the California Angels in 1995) and Hyannis' Jason Varitek (front center, selected by the Minnesota Twins in 1993 and Seattle Mariners in 1994). Boston Red Sox 1994 first-round pick Nomar Garciaparra also played in the All-Star game.Photo courtesy of Judy Scarafile.

out—but across the country. You get to see a foreign place, see a different part of the country, deal with different kinds of people."

CAPE BASEBALL SNAPSHOTS
The Recruiting of a Cape League Ballplayer

Shortly after the 1993 Cape League season, Yarmouth-Dennis general manager Jim Hagemeister sat down with his coaching staff. The Y-D Red Sox had finished one point out of the playoffs, but their pitching staff had been one of their strengths. Andy Taulbee posted a 7–2 mark, and finished with a 1.08 ERA. For his efforts, he copped the B.F.C. Whitehouse Award for being the league's top pitcher. In addition, Chris Clemons notched 10 saves, and was good enough to pick up the Robert McNeece Award as the league's outstanding pro prospect.

Hagemeister knew that they had to improve in each area, but would love to bolster his pitching staff with a blue-chip pitching prospect from the ACC or the Big East. With that extra pitcher, they could put themselves over the top.

The job of general manager entails working with the coaching staff, and finding players that you think would fit into the program. Hagemeister, along with Y-D manager John Barlowe and his assistant coaches, handled a good bit of the recruiting chores, but it wasn't easy.

"You need to get a verbal commitment from guys as soon as possible," Hagemeister said. "The other nine franchises are going to be out there recruiting and you've got other leagues around the country plus Team USA."

"The hard thing is, you don't have anything more to offer than anybody else. You can't offer them money, you can only offer them travel, a good housing situation and a good job. So the better you treat these kids when they come here, they're going to go back to school and say 'This is the franchise to go to.' So when you try to recruit a kid from that same school, it works to your benefit."

Early season Cape League contests tend to be pitchers' duels, as many of the players are still acclimating themselves to wooden bats. In addition, the chilly Cape evenings are tough for southern players who have been playing all year in warmer climates. Those two factors made good pitching valuable in the Cape League. Hagemeister knew that he could manuever his team into a playoff berth, with an extra pitcher or two making the difference.

He called his manager John Barlowe at Truett-McConnell College in Georgia and they discussed who they wanted to get next season.

The first name that came up was Florida State pitcher Jonathan Johnson. Johnson, a right-hander with excellent control, had been rated very highly by professional scouts.

Through the winter, Hagemeister had kept in contact with Johnson through his FSU pitching coach, Chip Baker. In early March, Hagemeister received a fateful phone call from Florida.

"Hey, Paul Wilson is looking for a place to play this summer," Baker said.

Hagemeister thought for a moment. Wilson was a big-time pitcher, the ace of one of the best collegiate pitching staffs in the country. In addition, the New York Mets were indicating that they were going to take Wilson with the number one pick in next June's amateur draft.

"Let me give you a call back," Hagemeister replied. He hung up and called Barlowe.

"We can get Paul Wilson," said Hagemeister.

"If you can grab him," Barlowe said, "grab him quickly."

As the season drew closer, Wilson's stock continued to rise. He was written up in *Sports Illustrated*'s "Inside Baseball" notebook as "having the look of a big leaguer—without the bonus baby mentality." One scout compared him to 1988 first pick Andy Benes, and was quoted as saying "I liked Andy then, and I do now. But I guarantee this kid will be much better."

Each team starts putting together their program book/media guide in the early spring. Inside, there are statistics from last year's club, a brief summary about what they do as a team for their town, advertising from local retailers, and pictures and statistics of each player on the team for the upcoming season. It is a convenient way to introduce to the players, and usually provides a large source of income for the club. The only problem is that rosters aren't set in stone. Players who appear in the roster book may never take the field for the team that season.

Hagemeister hoped that this wouldn't be the case when they placed Paul Wilson's picture and biography in the 1994 book. However, his biography hinted that he might not be spending a lot of time with Yarmouth-Dennis that summer: "Considered the best college pitcher in the country, Paul was the #1 player drafted by the Major Leagues this year. His fastball is consistently clocked at 92–95 mph, plus he has excellent control and fine command of an assortment of breaking pitches. His abilities indicate a highly successful professional career in the future."

The first week of June is a tough one for general managers on the Cape. They have to sweat out the major league draft. Hagemeister wasn't surprised when Wilson was made the number one pick by the pitching-poor Mets.

After they found out the results of the draft, Hagemeister called Wilson.

"I should know more about my situation this week," Wilson told him. "I'll definitely get back to you."

Later that week, Wilson called Yarmouth again. After exchanging pleasantries, Wilson broke the bad news.

"I'll be honest with you, Mr. Hagemeister. It looks like negotiations are going very well. I don't think I'll be coming to the Cape Cod League after all."

"That's okay," Hagemeister said, trying not to sound disappointed. "When will you know by for sure?"

"Probably Wednesday," Wilson replied.

"I'll get back to you Wednesday," Hagemeister replied, hoping for at least a Ben MacDonald-style cameo appearance that could give the Red Sox a shot in the arm.

Wednesday, Wilson called Hagemeister.

"We're probably going to sign this week," Wilson told him.

The chances of Wilson's appearance on the Cape were looking worse and worse.

Then, in the first week of the season, Hagemeister found out the bad news. He glumly sipped a cup of coffee behind home plate as the Red Sox faced Hyannis.

"I heard about it last night," Hagemeister told a reporter. "He's not coming down."

In addition to sitting down with the Mets that night, Wilson would be accepting an award in Houston later that same week. Otherwise, he would have been at Y-D for two weeks, tops.

Wilson and Hagemeister never even got a chance to meet. The entire series of negotiations had taken place over the phone.

"He was completely up front," Hagemeister said. "He said 'I don't want anything that anyone else isn't getting.' He just wanted be a regular player. I wish that every player that came up here was like him."

However, many athletes who don't reach a satisfactory agreement with the team that drafted them quite often head to Cape Cod to stay in shape. Number one pick Ben McDonald did it in 1989 with the Orleans Cardinals when he was negotiating with the Baltimore Orioles, but the most notable case might have been that of Jason Varitek. Drafted by the Astros out of high school in the late '80s, he decided to attend Georgia Tech, one of the top college baseball programs in the country. His strong arm behind the plate and his batting prowess made him legendary among professional scouts.

While at Georgia Tech, he quickly rose through the ranks to become one of the best college players in the country. After his junior season with the Yellow Jackets, he was drafted in the first round by the Minnesota Twins, who planned to have him catching at the major league level within a couple of years.

But his agent, Scott Boras, and the Twins couldn't come to an agreement. To stay in shape, Varitek decided to head to Cape Cod, where he had played the previous summer. He knew he could stay in top form while awaiting another, more lucrative contract offer from the Twins.

In his second tour of duty with Hyannis, he hit .371, with three homers and 22 RBI. Those numbers, along with his presence behind the plate, were enough to award him the league MVP award, along with the Thurman Munson award for the league's best batting average. And after turning down the Twins final offer of $450,000, he decided to return to Georgia Tech for his senior season.

One of only 10 two-time, first-round selections in the history
of baseball amateur draft, Georgia Tech catcher Jason Varitek
decided to gamble in the summer of 1993. He spurned a
$450,000 contract from the Minnesota Twins and played for
the Hyannis Mets instead, while waiting for a better offer.
It paid off, as the following year he was selected by the
Seattle Mariners. After a protracted negotiation,
he would eventually sign with Seattle.
Photo courtesy of Jack Aylmer.

Many professional baseball people scoffed at Varitek. What if he tore up a knee? In addition, many professional teams offer college seniors relatively low bonuses with a take-it-or-leave-it attitude, knowing that a ballplayer often has no choice but to sign. Where else could they go?

All Varitek did during his senior year was help Georgia Tech make it to the final game of the College World Series. He won the Howser Award as the nation's best college ballplayer during the 1994 season. *Baseball America* called him the "greatest catcher in college baseball history," and his coach credited his senior leadership with "willing Georgia Tech" to its first appearance in the College World Series. "He makes other players better because of how hard he works," said Tech head baseball coach Danny Hall.

The following June he was drafted as the 14th pick in the first round of the amateur draft by the Mariners. He held out once again, but eventually signed. He was one of only 10 two-time, first round draft picks in draft history.

Current Hyannis manager Steve Mrowka should know something about managing talented first-round picks. Over the last two years, he has managed three first-round picks: Varitek, Brian Buchanan, the 1994 first-round pick of the New York Yankees, and Carlton Loewer, the 1994 first-round pick of the Phillies. It is important that they bring a positive attitude to the team, says Mrowka, or they can really bring down team morale.

"When you get guys like them in here, it really depends on the makeup of the individual," Mrowka said. "If you get a kid in here who is just worried about making money, then he's going to be a detriment to the team. But we got Varitek in here, and he came in and worked hard, and helped work with the other ballplayers. The same was true with Buchanan and Loewer."

It wasn't likely, but maybe Varitek knew that he had history on his side. After the 1960 season, when he hit .352, Tommy Smith of Cotuit refused a contract with the New York Giants. The contract would have paid him a bonus of $12,500. But Smith returned to Holy Cross for his senior season. After receiving his degree, he signed and enjoyed a moderately successful major league career.

However, many times a holdout didn't go that well on Cape

Cod. Hartley Davis of the *Barnstable Patriot* once told the story of John Brown, perhaps "one of the greatest pitchers to toe the slab on a Cape diamond," according to Davis.

According to Davis, Brown was a star with Yale, and set to sign with the Yankees when he graduated. He would warm up just before game time, but if it was the least bit cool or damp, he would put his jacket on and simply sit on the bench, refusing to pitch. He felt that the weather might damage his arm, and the Yankees wanted him desperately.

Either the weather was so bad when he was in the Cape League or the Yankees didn't want him that badly. He never reached the major leagues.

But fortunately for the Mets (and unfortunately for the Cape League), there was none of that trouble with Wilson.

"I couldn't be happier with Paul Wilson," said John Barr, the Mets Director of Scouting. "He has the potential to be a very good major league pitcher. He's a horse, and I think the fans of New York will enjoy watching him pitch because of his attitude and the way he approaches the game."

"He didn't want to impose," Hagemeister said. "Heck, he could have imposed a little."

The Wilson and Varitek cases are extreme examples. Not every player is as sought after as they are. When a CCBL general manager has a thousand marginal role players lined up at his door, what kind of player does he look for?

"We don't just look for good ballplayers," said former Orleans GM and league president Dave Mulholland. "More important to all of us is what kind of kids are they? If you get positive kids, who come from solid programs and good, solid backgrounds, they're going to gel and play well together.

"You're always going to get kids who are going to come into the situation who have been the head honcho, whether it has been Little League, high school, Babe Ruth, or even at their college. And then they come in here and play a week and they look around and say 'Hey, wait a second. I'm just one of 20 guys here. I'm not the big shot anymore.

"I think it's a humbling experience for some of them. I think it's a real positive learning experience for many of them. And I think that's good for all of them."

PART III

Town by Town

Bourne Braves/Canalmen
(also Sagamore Clouters and Otis AFB)

"Whoever wants to know the heart and mind of America had better learn baseball, the rules and realities of the game — and do it by watching first some high school or small town teams."
— French philosopher Jacques Barzun

"It was a great time. I wouldn't have traded it for anything."
— Noel Kinski, 1965 Sagamore Clouters

CCBL Members: Sagamore — 1946–1965; Bourne-1934–39, 1961–69, 1971–72, 1988–Present; Otis AFB-1955, 1957–59, 1963–64.
CCBL Championships: Sagamore-1951, 1954, 1956, 1959, 1965; Bourne-None; Otis AFB-None.
Noted Major League Alumni: Noel Kinski (Bourne '64, Sagamore '65), Bob Schaefer (Sagamore '65), John Dockery (Sagamore '65), Mark Johnson ('88, '89), Bob Higginson ('91).
Field Location: Coady School Field on Trowbridge Road.
Team Records

		Manager	Finish
1965	25–9 (Sagamore)	n/a	2nd place
1966	17–17 (Sagamore)	n/a	5th place
1967	12–27 (Bourne)	n/a	6th place
1968	20–20 (Bourne)	Rick Doherty	4th place
1969	13–30 (Bourne)	Rick Doherty	8th place
1970	No team		

		Manager	Finish
1971	16–25 (Bourne)	Bob Schaefer	7th place
1972	14–25 (Bourne)	Bob Schaefer	7th place
1973-87 No team			
1988	12–29	Jim Watkins	5th place, West
1989	24–17–3	Jim Watkins	1st, West — lost in playoffs
1990	19–24–1	Bob Gendron	4th place, West
1991	20–20–4	Bob Gendron	4th place, West
1992	19–23–1	Bob Gendron	3rd place, West
1993	15–28–1	Bob Gendron	5th place, West
1994	12–28–3	Nino Giarrantano, Bob Stead	5th, West
1995	18–23–3	Bob Stead	4th, West
1996	18–25–1	Bob Stead	5th, West
1997	25–17–2	Kevin O'Sullivan	2nd, West — lost in playoffs

Player Records

Batting Average:	Harry Nelson	1964	.390
Home Runs:	Tom Smith	1969	10
Runs Batted In:	Tom Smith	1969	32
Stolen Bases:	Mike Basse	1990	28
ERA:	Winston Wheeler	1989	0.67
Wins:	Noel Kinski	1965	10
Strikeouts:	John Caniera	1972	119
Saves:	Winston Wheeler	1989	7

The years 1964 and 1965 were eventful ones for "Baseball at the Bridge." The Sagamore teams had been the toast of the CCBL in the '50s, winning four league championships between 1951 and 1959. At the same time, they had incurred the wrath of many local baseball players because they were the first team to actively recruit players from around the country, breaking the long standing but unwritten rule that only Cape natives were to play in the Cape League.

But the Clouters staggered in the early '60s. While Sagamore was the first team to recruit players from around the nation, it was Cotuit that made it an art. The Cotuit Kettleers won four straight championships, dominating the league between 1961 and 1964. Nevertheless, the start of the 1964 season saw three Cape League teams all within a long fly ball from the Cape Cod Canal: Otis AFB, Sagamore and Bourne.

The Otis AFB Minutemen didn't fare well during the 1964 campaign and were stumbling toward the finish. One day, late in the season, they didn't have enough players to start a game with Orleans. They forfeited the game and were consequently expelled from the league, never to return.

But while Otis AFB folded, the other two teams thrived. Led by pitcher Noel Kinski (who went 10–1), the Sagamore Clouters took the title. Kinski's record was so dominating that it stood for 22 years.

During that time, great pitchers such as Ron Darling, Charles Nagy, Mike Henneman, John Franco, Bob Tewksbury, Kirk McCaskill, Jeff Reardon and Kevin Tapani all entered the league, and all left without challenging Kinski's mark. Not until Pat Hope won 11 games for the 1987 Hyannis Mets was the record broken.

"It's not only the wins, but what made it tough to break that record was the fact that when you come in here, you only get 10 or 11 starts," reflected Kinski in 1994. "I think I was fortunate that I got that. Again, you only get 10 or 11 starts. You've got to win every one of them. It helped that I had a good club behind me."

He pitched for Bourne in 1964, for Sagamore in 1965, and Falmouth in 1966. He was the number one starter with both Sagamore and Falmouth and helped them both to win Cape League crowns. Many also remember him as one of the toughest pitchers of the era. He set a league record for complete games — 11 — that stood until 1987. In addition, his appearance in both ends of a doubleheader was bound to boost his reputation.

"I pitched the first game, and we lost to Cotuit," he recalled with a smile. "It was a tough loss, 5–3. The second game was also pretty close, and I came in. It was tied, or something. The manager asked me 'Jeez, can you come in and relieve? We need you to try and get a couple of left-handed guys out.'

"I ended up walking one guy. That guy ended up scoring, and it ended up being the winning run. It wasn't a lot of fun at the time, but it was one of those experiences that you go through when you're a pitcher."

The winter of 1964–65 saw the merger of the Sagamore and Bourne teams. It eliminated scheduling problems, as both teams used Keith Memorial Field. It was also a cost-cutting move for the town, slicing its operating budget almost in half. As a result, the 1965 Sagamore team was an impressive one, featuring Kinski, short-stop Bob Schaefer (currently the minor league coordinator with the Boston Red Sox), and part-time first baseman John Dockery (former New York Jet and current NBC college football analyst).

"We just played well together," Kinski recalls. "I don't know if we were necessarily, on paper, the best team, man-for-man, but I think we had a bunch of guys that really hung tough, played good defense, and won tight games. It was just a great experience."

But just as quickly as things took off, they crashed to earth again. Due to severe financial problems in the early '70s, there was no real continuity to the baseball teams in the Bourne/Sagamore area. Many years, teams would play entire seasons on the brink of bankruptcy, not sure if they were going to be able to afford to field a team the following summer. Nonetheless, Tom Cahir, who had a chance to play on the 1971 Bourne Canalmen squad under Bob Schaefer, said that uncertainty never affected their on-field performance.

"I didn't get the sense that the team was in financial trouble when I played there," Cahir said. "From what I saw as a player, it was well supported. Before I was of that age, when I was just a kid, I knew that there was a Sagamore team and a Bourne team, and they were well supported. I saw the same thing in the early '70s."

Soon after that, entrepreneur Ted Turner was close to donating lights to the field at the Massachusetts Maritime Academy. According to Jack Aylmer, who had a hand in awarding Turner an honorary degree from the MMA, the subject was broached between the two gentlemen over dinner at the Captain's Table in Hyannis. However, all that came of it was a few exhibition games against the Citadel, where Turner's son was a student.

"Baseball by the Bridge" had a whole new meaning when the Bourne Braves moved into Hendy Field at Massachusetts Maritime Academy in the late ´80s. The old railroad bridge that spans the Cape Cod Canal is seen in the background. Hendy Field served as the home of the Braves until 1997, when the Braves moved into their new digs behind the Coady School in Bourne. Photo courtesy of Bob Corradi.

However, Aylmer wasn't deterred. He decided to award an honorary degree to George Steinbrenner. Despite Steinbrenner's troubles with baseball (he had recently been kicked out of the game for his association with gambler Howie Spira), Aylmer pushed for and won the opportunity for Steinbrenner to speak at the commencement ceremony.

At the time, Stump Merrill was the Yankees manager, and Buck Showalter was managing the Yankees Triple-A affiliate in Columbus, Ohio. Aylmer was close to Showalter from his time in the Cape League when Showalter played at Hyannis and stayed with the Aylmer family.

Aylmer ended up giving Steinbrenner a ride back to the airport in Hyannis from Buzzards Bay. Aylmer found out that Steinbrenner wouldn't be able to provide the money necessary for lights, but other baseball topics came up during the ride, Showalter among them.

Aylmer asked why Showalter wasn't managing the Yankees.

"I tell you, just between you and I," Steinbrenner said confidentially. "Bucky Showalter came about that close" — Steinbrenner held his fingers about one-sixteenth of an inch apart — "to being the manager instead of Stump Merrill. But if there is ever another chance, he'll make it."

In the fall of 1994, the Bourne Braves broke ground on a new field. The old, abandoned baseball field at the Coady School on Trowbridge Road was turned into a state-of-the-art facility, complete with irrigation, dugouts, press box and scoreboard.

To pay for the field, Bourne town officials divided the area into a grid, and sold parcels of the field for $5. While the town is the owner and operator of the facility, the Braves, Senior Babe Ruth and the high school soccer team all divide the use. Investors purchasing the property could request certain positions on the baseball or soccer field (if a certain area had already been purchased, the organizers tried to get as close as possible). In addition, they received "deeds" for their purchases, with the intention that it would make them feel a part of the rebirth of exciting, competitive baseball at the bridge.

Brewster Whitecaps

"I played for two years on the Cape, and at the time, it was, by far, the best competition I had faced. Brewster was fun, and the Cape used the wood bats that really gave me a jump start on pro ball." —Damon Buford, 1989 Brewster Whitecaps

CCBL Members: 1988–Present
CCBL Championships: None
Noted Major League Alumni: Dave Staton ('88), F.P. Santangelo ('88), Damon Buford ('89), Billy Wagner ('92), Todd Walker ('92).
Field Location: Cape Cod Tech Field, Route 124, Harwich. Yep, you read that right—Harwich. Cape Tech is located on Route 124 in Harwich, just north of exit 10 on Route 6. The field is wedged into a back corner of other athletic fields, with four sets of bleachers that run along the first base and right field lines. Parking is available in the Cape Tech lot.

Team Records

		Manager	Finish
1988	17–25	Joe Walsh	5th place, East
1989	22–20–2	Rolando Casanova	2nd, East—lost in playoffs*
1990	23–20	Rolando Casanova	3rd place, East
1991	21–22–1	Darren Mazeroski	3rd place, East
1992	26–18	John Hughes	2nd, East—lost in playoffs
1993	23–20–1	Elliot Avent	3rd place, East

Since their inception in 1988, the Brewster Whitecaps have
played at Harwich's Cape Tech Field.
Photo by Michelle Adams.

		Manager	**Finish**
1994	24–18–1	Bill Mosiello	2nd, East — lost in finals
1995	17–25–1	Steve Rousey	4th, East
1996	23–20–1	Bill Mosiello	1st, East — lost in playoffs
1997	22–22–0	Bill Mosiello	3rd in West

*Brewster and Chatham finished in a tie for second place. Brewster defeated Chatham in a one-game playoff.

Player Records

Batting Average: (wood bats)	Dave Staton	1988	.359
Home Runs:	Dave Staton	1988	16
Runs Batted In:	Dave Staton	1988	46
Stolen Bases:	Darrell Nicholas	1992	40
ERA:	Garvin Alston	1991	1.76
Wins:	Rich Greene	1990	8
Saves:	Mike Sciortino	1989	4
	Chris Harrigan	1993	4

The town of Brewster had a fervor for the game of baseball as far back as 1937, when records indicate that they had at least one team in one of the many twilight leagues. The main ballfield was in front of the Brewster school on Main Street where the town offices are now, but there was a second field that was almost always in use on Lower Road. Known as Thorndike Park, it is close to the bay beach, near what is known as Paine's Creek today.

It wasn't just at the semipro level that Brewster enjoyed success on the diamond. In 1938, the high school team fielded all the boys in the school. Even so, the efforts of the ten players were still enough to give them the Cape high school crown.

The Brewster teams of the late '40s and early '50s were like the present-day club, teams that concentrated on speed and defense to win games. Ballplayers such as the Gage brothers (John, Tommy, Jim and Ernie, the latter of whom would sign with the White Sox) helped keep the team competitive throughout the '50s.

Besides the Gage brothers, there were many other memorable ballplayers. Billy Latham is remembered for hitting a ball over a house on the opposite side of Main Street. His brother John was also skilled at the plate. Maurice Lee, who hit .600 one summer in Brewster, according to one former teammate, signed a minor league deal with the Washington Senators.

The Brewster team played until 1959, when they dropped out of the league. In 1988, the town was awarded its first franchise of the modern era. The name "Whitecaps" was suggested in 1987 by Brewster native William Turkington, who said that he got the idea "from watching the whitecaps on Cape Cod Bay." Of the 146 name entries submitted, it was the one the team's executive committee settled on.

However, many in the Harwich franchise were wary about Brewster moving into their area. They received assurances at that time that one of the conditions for the acceptance of the Brewster franchise in 1988 was that the field location was to be a "temporary" residence at Cape Cod Tech. There were plans to renovate the field in front of the old Brewster Elementary School, the field that was used by the Brewster teams of the ´40s and ´50s.

But the stipulation, originally pushed for by the Harwich franchise, was later dropped. And, despite occasional troubles with Cape Tech about establishing a permanent outfield fence and terracing the first base hill to make it easier for elderly fans, things aren't all bad. After all, the school's top-notch horticultural program allows the field to stay a deep, lush green throughout the entire season.

Since their reappearance in 1988, the Whitecaps have remained consistently competitive, through celebrity appearances as well as some good old-fashioned exciting baseball. In 1988, Kevin McHale, who was also part-owner of the Brewster resort Ocean Edge, threw out the first pitch on "Ocean Edge Appreciation Night," and Hall of Famers Harry "The Hat" Walker and Stan Musial helped out with batting tips that season. Red Sox broadcaster Bob Montgomery also made an appearance to root for the Whitecaps.

A permanent electronic scoreboard replaced the hand-operated model during the 1994 season, and a permanent fence was also added, giving the field a more professional look.

Chatham A's

*"I came out of a small school with not much confidence and hit a
whopping .208 for Chatham my first year. But I think I learned
by the end of the year that I had a chance to be as good as those
guys. That really helped my confidence."*

— Jeff Bagwell, 1987 and 1988 Chatham A's

CCBL Members: 1923–31,* 1946–Present
(*denotes a shared franchise in 1927 with Harwich)
CCBL Championships: 1967, 1982, 1992, 1996
Noted Major League Alumni: Charlie Hough (´64), Tom Grieve
(´66), Thurman Munson (´67), Mike Pagliarulo (´80), Kevin Seitzer
(´82), Marvin Freeman, Bobby Witt (´83), Joey Cora (´84), Albert
Belle (´86), Jeff Bagwell (´87–´88)
Field Location: Veterans Field, Depot Station, Chatham Center.
This cozy park is situated right off of Route 28 in Chatham center.
The field is ringed with bleachers high above the playing field from
dugout-to-dugout. The entire outfield is banked beyond the fence,
which runs from 340' down the left field line to 385' to center and
320' away to right field. Not many home run hitters come out of
Chatham, as the heavy fog often takes the power out of a long
drive.

All home games start at 7 P.M. But if your kids aren't into baseball, there is a large playground down the right field line.

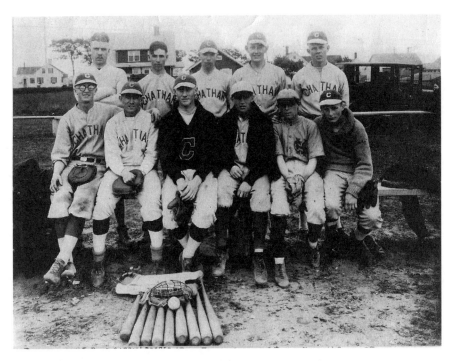

Baseball has always been successful in Chatham. This picture of the 1924 Chatham High team was taken at one of several fields in town prior to World War II, probably the one at the corner of Barcliff and Old Harbor Road.
Photo courtesy of Tom Desmond.

Team Records

		Manager	Finish
1965	25–7	n/a	1st place
1966	30–4	n/a	1st place
1967	30–9	n/a	1st place
1968	17–23	n/a	6th place
1969	29–15	Joe Lewis	1st place
1970	21–20	Doug Holmquist	5th place
1971	18–22–2	Ben Hays	5th place
1972	25–17	Ben Hays	4th place
1973	26–14–1	Ben Hays	1st place
1974	19–23	Ben Hays	5th place
1975	16–25–1	Joe Russo	6th place
1976	30–11–1	Ed Lyons	1st place
1977	25–16–1	Ed Lyons	2nd place
1978	25–17	Ed Lyons	2nd place
1979	19–21–2	Ed Lyons	4th place
1980	29–13	Ed Lyons	1st place
1981	15–27	Ed Lyons	8th place
1982	20–21–1	Ed Lyons	4th place
1983	15–25–2	John Mayotte	7th place
1984	18–23–1	John Mayotte	6th place
1985	31–10–1	John Mayotte	1st, lost in championship
1986	22–19–1	John Mayotte	4th, lost in playoffs
1987	17–25	John Mayotte	6th place
1988	19–24	Bob Whalen, Jr.	4th place, East
1989	22–20–2	Bob Whalen, Jr.	2nd, East*
1990	17–24–2	Rich Hill	5th place, East
1991	24–19–1	Rich Hill	1st, East — won title
1992	31–11	Rich Hill	1st, East — won title
1993	25–19	Hill, John Schiffner	1st, East — lost in playoffs

1994	16–25–2	John Schiffner	4th place, East
1995	25–17–1	John Schiffner	1st place, East — lost in championship
1996	22–21–1	John Schiffner	2nd place, East — lost in championship
1997	22–22–0	John Schiffner	2nd place, East — lost in playoffs

*Brewster and Chatham ended the season tied for 2nd place. Brewster defeated Chatham in a one-game playoff.

Player Records

Batting Average:	Tim McIntosh	1985	.392
Home Runs:	Albert Belle	1986	12
Runs Batted In:	Glenn Davis	1980	44
Stolen Bases:	Jeremy Carr	1992	47
ERA:	Steve Duda	1992	0.91
Wins:	Matt Williams	1991	8
Strikeouts:	Mike Whitley	1993	85
Saves:	Chris Lee	1985	9

The consensus among Cape League fans is that the top three ballparks in the league are located in Orleans, Cotuit, and Chatham. The Chatham boosters feel strongly about their ballpark, built in the late 1940s and named after the Chatham veterans who served in World War II.

On the backstop, there is a plaque placed in memory of the late John H. Shepard, a baseball fan and supporter of the Chatham Twilight League that was placed there in the 1940s. It reads: "In memory of John H. Shepard. 1876–1939. A true sportsman. Erected by the Chatham Baseball Team."

Prior to Veterans Field, the Chatham franchise played some of their games in the vicinity of Barcliff and Old Harbor Roads. It was a ballpark without an outfield fence, and was surrounded by woods. According to longtime Chatham fan Tom Desmond, the Chatham team would occasionally use this to their advantage. They would hide baseballs in the woods, and if a ball was hit deep into the forest and they were unable to find it, they would simply grab the hidden one and toss that back into play.

The pride of the town and the team is evident as soon as you arrive for a night game. At dusk, the sun sets beyond the tree line in deep left center field. People in the know get to the game early and pull into the parking spaces beyond the right field line, so they can watch the sunset as the first few innings get underway. The two scoreboards allow a fan to see the score and the count from any seat in the ballpark. A series of wooden bleachers stretches from first base around towards third, and the press box and announcer's booth sits on top of the stands between third and home.

No less an authority than Peter Gammons, the most influential baseball writer in the country, considers Veterans Field the finest on the Cape.

"I love that ballpark," Gammons says wistfully. "There is just something so perfect about that place."
One of the first managers of the modern era in Chatham was Joe "Skippy" Lewis, who was also a friend to many, including long-time CCBL umpire Curly Clement, who rates him as the number one manager in his 33 years in the league.

"Skippy was the best coach that I ever worked with," Clement said. "He was tremendous when it came to recruiting, but he was also a good teacher and a good baseball man."

"In those days Joe Lewis and the Chatham franchise had a lot of money behind them," said Dick Bresciani, who was in charge of PR for the league in the late '60s. "Joe's father was a major league scout, so he had a lot of contacts, and could bring in players from all over. That forced many of the other clubs to either start doing the same thing, or fall by the wayside. And that's when Livesey in Falmouth and Williams in Orleans and Arnold Mycock of Cotuit would scout players throughout the spring to keep up with Joe Lewis and the people of Chatham."

A lot of the official team business in those early days was conducted by the Chatham Athletic Association in Willard Nicholas' Barber Shop, located on Chatham's Main Street, across from the Wayside Inn.

"Everyone would congregate at Nick's," recalls former Chatham president Tom Desmond. "The players would all report there when they arrived on the Cape. We received team mail there.

It was the unofficial headquarters for the Chatham A's for many years."

Nicholas was a longtime supporter of the A's, whether it was announcing games from the press box in the 1970s or organizing the first merchandising booth at Veterans Field in 1993. He faithfully served the Chatham Athletic organization for 28 years, and was also Chairman of the Chatham Recreation Department for 14 years. Many believe it is unlikely that Nicholas ever missed a game until his death in 1994.

One of the first stars of the league as it entered the modern era was Thurman Munson. During his time with the Chatham A's, the then-Kent State catcher was known as one of the most talkative backstops in the league.

"He was always jabbering away at these guys when they came up to bat," recalled Bresciani. "He had kind of a slow, southern drawl, even though he wasn't really from the South. With him, it was always 'Hey, kid. You think yer' gonna get a hit? We're gonna blow this one right by you.' He was always jabbering away at these guys."

And it was Munson who suffered perhaps the most embarassing injury in Chatham history. In the process of leading the league with a .420 mark for Chatham in the summer of 1967, he hit a deep drive to right field one night with two runners on. After it cleared the fence, Munson went into his home run trot. With his teammates waiting for him at home plate, he jumped into their arms, ready to celebrate the big homer. In so doing, he tripped over home plate and sprained his ankle. It's unsure how much time he spent on the bench as a result of the injury, but many who were at Veterans Field that night say that the only thing that hurt worse than his ankle was his pride.

One of the proudest moments for the Chatham ballpark in recent years was the hosting of the 1984 clash between that year's Olympic squad and a team of CCBL all-stars. Former league president Dick Sullivan remembers:

"We decided to really do it right, and leave nothing to the imagination," Sullivan said. "It started with a full-blown clambake, just a huge cookout. Richard Costello of the Chatham Squire offered a

Former league president and commissioner Dick Sullivan
(right) and 1984 U.S. Olympic baseball coach Rod Dedeaux
(center) spend time with a young fan at the Chatham Bars Inn
before the 1984 Olympic baseball team faced a collection of
Cape League All-Stars. Dedeaux called his time on the Cape
the most enjoyable part of his pre-Olympic tour.
Photo courtesy of Dick Sullivan.

free meal. I had every local politician looking to throw out the first pitch. The Chatham band was there, and the players exchanged gifts before the game. We had speakers and all kinds of other ceremonies."

Former Cape Leaguers such as Will Clark and Billy Swift returned to the Cape before heading out to Los Angeles for the Olympics later that summer. The Cape League put the players up at a local hotel, and treated them to a pre-game meal at the Chatham Bars Inn.

While all was well off the field, Cape League officials were worried about the on-field discrepancy in talent. Even though the Cape League was already established as the premier summer college league in the nation, they were facing the best collegians in America. "We didn't want to be embarrassed," Sullivan said. "But you looked in that Team USA dugout and it was a showcase of talent. We were just saying to ourselves 'Let's make it close.'"

With a huge crowd in attendance, the Olympians were duly impressed. And as for the contest, it was clear that the game was closer than the Olympians had anticipated. The Cape Leaguers took a 3–2 lead into the ninth inning, but Oddibe McDowell hit a shot that bounced on the road past the right field fence and into the fire station, allowing the Olympians to take a dramatic 4–3 victory. But the memory will live on long after the final score has been forgotten.

"Rod Dedeaux said that Team USA's time on the Cape was the most enjoyable part of their pre-Olympic tour," Sullivan said. "It was a lot of work, and it didn't cost the league one penny."

Cotuit Kettleers

"I wouldn't have made it to the majors if it hadn't been for my experience playing with Cotuit in the Cape League. Playing there definitely helped me because the league is well-scouted, and it gave me a chance to be noticed."

— Jeff Reardon, 1976 Cotuit Kettleers

CCBL Members: 1947–Present
CCBL Championships: 1961, 1962, 1963, 1964, 1972, 1973, 1974, 1975, 1977, 1981, 1984, 1985, 1995.
Noted Major League Alumni: Jeff Reardon ('76), Tim Teufel ('79), Ron Darling, John Franco ('80), Terry Steinbach ('81–'82), Will Clark ('83), Joe Girardi ('84), Greg Vaughn ('85), Ed Sprague ('86), Tim Naehring ('87), Jeff Kent, Tim Salmon, Dan Wilson ('88), Scott Erickson ('89), Jermaine Allensworth ('92)
Field Location: Lowell Park, Lowell Street, Cotuit. The *Cape Cod Times* has called it a "diamond ringed in emerald." Lowell Park is located less than two miles south of Route 28 in Cotuit. The small parking lot fills quickly for home games, but cars also park on Lowell and Putnam Avenues and Main Street.

The Kettleers probably take the award for having the most unique name in CCBL history. According to the 1994 Cotuit yearbook, Ed Semprini, former sports editor of the *New Bedford Standard-Times* and current columnist for the *Barnstable Patriot*, helped coin the name after referring to the Cotuit ball club as the Kettleers in his coverage of the Cape Cod League games. According to legend, more than 300 years ago the Indians bartered with

159

the early settlers for the land on which the villages of Cotuit and Santuit now stand. The terms of payment were a brass kettle, with a hoe thrown in for good measure.

Team Records

Year	Record	Manager	Finish
1965	15–16	Jim Hubbard	6th place
1966	14–22	Jim Hubbard	6th place
1967	22–16	Jim Hubbard	3rd place
1968	16–24	Jim Hubbard	7th place
1969	21–22	Jim Hubbard	4th place
1970	23–19	Jack McCarthy	4th place
1971	20–18–4	Jack McCarthy	4th place-lost in playoffs
1972	26–15–1	Jack McCarthy	1st place — won title
1973	24–17	Jack McCarthy	2nd place — won title
1974	20–19–3	Jack McCarthy	4th place — won title
1975	24–18	Jack McCarthy	3rd place — won title
1976	25–12–5	Jack McCarthy	2nd place — lost in playoffs
1977	27–13–1	Jack McCarthy	1st place — won title
1978	19–22–1	Jack McCarthy	6th place
1979	23–17–2	George Greer	2nd place — lost in playoffs
1980	25–15–2	George Greer	3rd place — lost in playoffs
1981	19–18–5	George Greer	4th place — won title
1982	24–16–2	George Greer	2nd place — lost in playoffs
1983	27–11–3	George Greer	1st — lost in championship
1984	22–16–4	George Greer	3rd place — won title
1985	28–14	George Greer	2nd place — won title
1986	23–18–1	George Greer	2nd — lost in championship
1987	22–18	George Greer	4th place — lost in playoffs
1988	21–18	Pete Varney	3rd place, West
1989	23–20–1	Pete Varney	3rd place, West

		Manager	**Finish**
1990	22–19–2	Roger Bidwell	2nd, West — lost in playoffs
1991	21–21–2	Roger Bidwell	3rd place, West
1992	28–14–1	Roger Bidwell	1st, West — lost in championship
1993	24–20	Roger Bidwell	3rd place, West
1994	20–21–2	Roger Bidwell	4th place, West
1995	29–11–3	Mike Coutts	1st, West — won champ.
1996	23–19–2	Mike Coutts	3rd place, West
1997	21–21–2	Tom Walters	4th place, West

Player Records

Batting Average:	Terry Steinbach	1982	.431
Home Runs:	Tim Teufel	1979	16
Runs Batted In:	Steinbach	1982	54
Stolen Bases:	Greg Lotzar	1983	33
ERA:	n/a		
Wins:	Joseph Pursell	1980	8
Saves:	Todd Marion	1991	11

At the turn of the century, baseball in Cotuit was played mostly at Crocker's Field, located on what would later become the Santuit Golf Links. The location is now the site of "Kings Grant," off Old Kings Road in Cotuit. Over the years, recreational baseball had been played in Cotuit, but the small village (one of the seven villages of Barnstable) would have to wait for entry into the Cape Cod League until after World War II.

The Kettleers currently play in Lowell Park, named after Elizabeth Lowell, the wife of the former President of Harvard University, Abbot Lawrence Lowell, who summered in Cotuit for many years. In fact, Cotuit was home to so many Harvard people that they once pondered changing the town's name to "Little Harvard." The Lowells donated the land to the town of Barnstable for school purposes in 1906. The Elizabeth Lowell High School stood on the front parcel until 1926, and the old school foundation can still be found in the wooded section of the west side of the present parking lot.

However, the dimensions of the playing field in those early

years were quite a bit different than they are today. Right field was practically a sand pit, and stood much lower than the rest of the outfield. There were no fences or dugouts. There was a low backstop, made of wood and chicken wire, and a small wooden grandstand stretched down the third base line. There was an all-dirt infield.

Despite the relatively small size of Cotuit, they were a fiercely competitive team on the field. They fielded a team in the Barnstable Recreation Commission Twi-Light League in 1946 that was made up of many players and coaches who went on to success in the Cape League in the ʹ50s and ʹ60s. Local players included Howie and Eddie Bearse, Pete Pells, Jr., Dick Behlman, Dave Fish, Bob Lorange, and Jim Irwin, all under the age of 17. Coaching the club were Edson Scudder, Cal Burlingame and Vic Robello.

The poor quality of the field soon stood in contrast to the high level of play. It was obvious that the field needed to be upgraded. In 1952, the infield was seeded, and the outfield was bulldozed to its present dimensions. Soon after that, outfield fences were constructed, dugouts were built, an open-air press box was added, and a larger grandstand was erected.

As the Kettleers established themselves as the class of the CCBL throughout the ʹ50s and ʹ60s, the field and facilities surrounding it were renovated accordingly. The original dugouts, built in 1951, were replaced in 1964, the same year that a sprinkler system was installed in the infield. In 1965, restrooms were built, and 1966 saw the paving of the parking lot. The following year, the press box was built and the first electronic scoreboard was installed.

In 1981, *Sports Illustrated* came to Cape Cod during the major league players' strike to write a story about other brands of baseball that were still going on. An accompanying photo essay included a two-page aerial photograph of Lowell Park that currently hangs in the Cotuit library. The following year, a new press box and games sales booth were built by Kettleer volunteers. The field has remained the same since the 1982 changes, but is still considered to be, along with Chatham and Orleans, one of the most beautiful ballparks on the Cape.

And Cotuit's outstanding field has been matched with some

of the most peerless play in the history of the Cape. The Kettleers have set the standard dating back to the earliest days of the league.

Even though Cotuit didn't officially enter the Cape League until 1947, there is a great history of baseball in the Barnstable/Cotuit area. It is believed that baseball was played at Cotuit as early as 1883, when the *Barnstable Patriot* carried the account of a 25–11 win by Cotuit over rival Osterville. The *Patriot* went on to say that a "brilliant audience of young ladies, and others, added very much interest" to the game.

In the '40s, the town of Barnstable supported its recreational teams (Hyannis, Osterville, and Cotuit) by granting $900 to be shared by the teams to purchase uniforms and equipment. Cotuit added to its income by passing the hat. According to contemporary reports, five to ten dollars was considered a generous donation. And the fans came to see players such as Matt "Pete" Pells, Roger Burlingame, Stan "Bones" Turner, Osborne Bearse, and Clarence Fish, who became legendary in the tiny village for their ballplaying ability.

When the Mashpee team folded in the mid-'50s, many of the players joined the Cotuit team, helping to make it one of the best in the Upper Cape. Brothers Vern and Ollie Pocknett, Fred Peters, Don Hicks, Jimmy Cash (a rarity in baseball — a left-handed second baseman) and Earl Mills were added to the Cotuit roster. Local players who were also added through the early '50s included the Robellos (Vic, Manny and Joe), the Scudders (Edson and Roger), the Crockers (Lee and Harry), Jim Perkins and Cal Burlingame. All of these players helped set the tone for the on-the-field excellence that was to follow. For example, the top-notch hitting of Big Jim Perkins caught the notice of "Ripley's Believe It or Not" in the mid-'60s when he smacked two grand slams in one inning. Even though Ripley's said it was three, Cotuit didn't need any help from the scorekeeper, as they triumphed by a 28–3 count. The game was called after five innings.

Continuity also seemed to be important to the Cotuit franchise. While many of the other franchises had players, managers and front office people come and go, Cotuit kept the same people in place year after year. Roger Scudder managed the club in the late '40s and early '50s. He was succeeded by Cal Burlingame, who later handed the reins over to Eddie Bearse. Paul Thomas of West Barnstable finished out the '50s as the Cotuit manager.

Off the field, Cotuit set the pace financially. The Cotuit Athletic Association was formed in 1950, allowing the team to raise funds through activities such as the annual Quahog Chowder Supper, held in Cotuit's Bruce Hall. For 75 cents, you could get chowder (with seconds), tossed salad, apple pie and coffee, and support the Kettleers at the same time.

Much of the credit for seeing that Cotuit became successful belonged to Arnold Mycock. Mycock had been with the Kettleers since 1950, and had quickly developed a reputation as a tireless worker. A September 1960 article in the *Barnstable Patriot*, shortly after the Kettleers won the first of four consecutive titles, said the following: "The success of the Cotuit team was due in no little part to the efforts of Arnie Mycock. Arnie puts in a lot of time, not only during the season but before and after. In fact, he works 12 months out of the year for that team."

Mycock assumed the role of general manager soon after he arrived, and hasn't stopped working since. With his support, Cotuit began actively recruiting players in 1960. Several major league teams were contacted to help, and the Philadelphia Phillies and New England scout George Owen responded. The Phillies donated some equipment (bats and baseballs), and recommended a manager. Cotuit took the advice, and Gene Savard, a former allstar at Middleboro High and one-time Canadian pro baseball player, became their player-manager.

Savard was an energetic man, but had a big test ahead of him. The Sagamore Clouters, who had won four Cape League titles in nine years, had already started recruiting players from around Massachusetts, picking up the best players from schools such as Bridgewater State and UMass. But Savard quickly caught up to them, going even farther afield throughout New England to select the best collegiate players. Savard wasn't afraid to take the field himself to show the players how it should be done. In his first game as Kettleer manager, Savard started Wayne Glover on the mound. After several strong innings, Glover began to tire with the bases loaded with only one out. Savard chose to face the crisis himself. The first batter he faced grounded back to the mound. Savard fielded the ball and got the force at home. The next batter popped up to the mound and Savard snatched it. The Kettleers held on to the lead, and took the victory.

1960 would be the first and final year for Savard, but it was just the beginning of the Cotuit dynasty. And as the '50s gave way to the '60s, the seeds that had been planted by general manager Arnold Mycock would blossom into fruition under new manager Jim Hubbard.

Using many players out of St. John's University in New York City, the 1961 Kettleers won the first of four consecutive Cape League titles. Under Hubbard, they were the class of the league. The 1964 team was probably one of the best in league history, finishing with a 31–3 mark and an 18-game win streak. Seven of the players on that club went on to play professional baseball.

"If that team had been playing today, they would have all been drafted," Mycock said.

As the Kettleers were enjoying success on the field, they were also enjoying success financially. They were the first team to become a corporation in 1962. Mycock remembers the move:

"That gave us a good vehicle for fundraising. We also had a lot of people who were really interested in that team. It was, and still is a small community, so we have many townsfolk working together, making it a success."

The second wave of the Cotuit dynasty began in 1970, when Jack McCarthy took over the Kettleers.

In 1970, McCarthy managed the sons of two Hall-of-Famers, Kevin Cronin and Larry Berra. The team finished in fourth place that year, and in 1971 they finished fourth again. But '71 saw several outstanding performances, including a no-hitter from lefty Rick Burley, who threw a 2–0 whitewashing of Harwich. In addition to Burley's impressive performance, left fielder John Varga of Seattle turned in an all-star performance by hitting .340 with 50 hits in 20 straight games. Pitcher Brian Sheekey of Rhode Island was also outstanding, striking out 96 batters in 96 innings.

But it was the following year that Cotuit enjoyed a return to

Cotuit GM Arnold Mycock (right) and manager Jim Hubbard
(center) accept the 1964 Upper Division Championship trophy
from league commissioner Danny Silva.
Photo courtesy of Arnold Mycock.

dominance. It would be the first of another four straight titles, and five in six years. Future major leaguers such as UMass righthander Jeff Reardon (1974–1975, 62 strikeouts in 76 innings pitched in 1974), Joe Beckwith (Los Angeles), and Sal Butera (Minnesota) were all instrumental in returning the Kettleers to championship status. But despite his big numbers with Cotuit, Reardon went almost unnoticed by major league scouts, mostly because of his attitude.

"He had a terrible temper," Mycock recalls. "It almost always got the better of him."

"I was young and cocky, and maybe some people didn't like my attitude," admitted Reardon. "Arnold Mycock helped me focus that wildness when I was on the mound."

After finishing up with the Kettleers, he went to play professional baseball in Canada. A scout from the New York Mets watched him throw, and called Mycock for a reference.

"What about Jeff Reardon?" asked the scout. "Should we take a chance on him?"

"He pitched every big game for us over the last few years," replied Mycock. "He's six-feet-one, weighs 200 pounds and can throw the ball through the wall. What more do you want?"

"Okay," replied the stunned scout. "How can I get hold of him?"

"He's staying with his girlfriend," Mycock said. "Let me give you his number."

Soon after that, he was in the major leagues with the Mets.

"If it wasn't for Arnold Mycock, I don't think the Mets would have signed me," Reardon said. "He would never admit it to me, but I think Arnold knew the scout pretty well and put in a good word. I owe a major debt to him for my major league career."

The 1977 Cotuit squad could have been one of the most talented teams in league history. They batted .312, and hit an amazing 50 home runs, a feat that will probably never be duplicated because the league switched back to wooden bats in 1985. They had the batting champion in left fielder Del Bender, home run and RBI leader Joe Reitano (who pulled double duty at both catcher and outfield), and hits leader Gary Redus in center field.

But the Kettleers faced an imposing presence in the league

Above: When Jeff Reardon (right) was honored by the Boston Red Sox for breaking the all-time major league saves record, Mycock (at podium) was there to share the honor. Reardon, who played for Cotuit, credits Mycock for helping jump-start his baseball career. *Below:* Cotuit's Arnold Mycock has been associated with baseball on Cape Cod since the 1940s. Photos courtesy of Arnold Mycock.

championship series in Yarmouth-Dennis. In the first year of the merger between the Yarmouth and Dennis teams, Y-D's Steve Balboni, who would finish in a tie with Cotuit's Brian Denman in the vote for the newly created Best Pro Prospect Award, blasted six home runs and drove in 16 runs over the course of the five-game championship series, but it wasn't enough to beat out the Kettleers, as they triumphed 8–3 in the fifth game of the series.

1978 saw the end of an era in Cotuit, as McCarthy handed over the reigns after his only losing season (19–22–1) and a sixth-place finish. He decided to pursue his doctoral degree in the field of guidance counseling, but he always recalls his time with the Kettleers with great fondness.

"Those were just great years," McCarthy told Cotuit team historian Stew Goodwin in 1994. "I think that from mid-July through the playoffs were some of the best times of my life."

The 1980s, with championships coming in 1981, 1984, 1985, were relatively uneventful. However, the classic players continued to parade through Lowell Park. Ron Darling, John Franco, Terry Steinbach, Greg Vaughn, Will Clark, Tim Naehring, Ed Sprague, Jeff Kent, and Tim Salmon all played for the Kettleers in the 1980s, and many of them enjoyed CCBL championships.

In the 1990s, Lowell Park was the site of a baseball landmark of a more literary sort. According to a report in the *Boston Globe,* famed author Norman Mailer broke a long-standing vow at a Cape League game in the summer of 1995. It seemed that Mailer, a rabid Brooklyn Dodgers fan, vowed never to attend another baseball game after the Dodgers left Brooklyn in 1957. However, the famed author broke his promise by taking in a Wareham-Cotuit game at Lowell Park in Cotuit that July.

But as the players keep coming and Cotuit keeps winning into the 1990s, Arnold Mycock remains the one constant when it comes to baseball in Cotuit.

"Year after year, teams will run into situations with players who go home unhappy," said John Claffey, who has known Mycock through the league for the last 20 years. "You never see that in Cotuit. Cotuit players come there to play, and they stay there, and that stems directly from Arnold Mycock. He is a very, very respected professional."

Falmouth Commodores

"That summer in Falmouth, it was the first time I had been away from home, so that helped me grow as a person. It was the first time I had used the wood bat, and I was facing some of the top competition in the country, so it helped me grow as a player. It was great being on my own in a different part of the country."
— Tino Martinez, 1986 Falmouth Commodores

CCBL Members: 1923–Present
CCBL Championships: 1923, 1929, 1931, 1932, 1935, 1938, 1939, 1946, 1966, 1968, 1969, 1970, 1971, 1980
Noted Major League Alumni: Steve Balboni ('76), Tony Fossas ('78), Sid Bream ('80), Kevin Tapani ('85), Tino Martinez ('86), Steven "Turk" Wendell ('87), Darin Erstad ('93, '94).
Field Location: Guv Fuller Field, Main Street, Falmouth Center. Located right behind the Falmouth police station and the Gus Canty Community Center on Route 28 in Falmouth center, Fuller Field is one of two fields that doubles as a football facility (Wareham is the other). The paved parking lot next door allows for plenty of parking, and the lights allow for all home games to start 7 P.M. There is a large set of bleachers along the home dugout, and a smaller section of bleachers along the visitor's side. There is also an area to stand alongside the major league scouts behind the plate.
Team Records

		Manager	Finish
1965	17–15	n/a	4th place
1966	20–14	n/a	2nd place

		Manager	Finish
1967	28–12	n/a	2nd place
1968	26–14	Bill Livesey	2nd place
1969	26–18	Bill Livesey	3rd place
1970	25–16	Bill Livesey	1st place
1971	30–12	Bill Livesey	1st place—won title
1972	26–15–1	Bill Livesey	2nd place—lost in playoffs
1973	16–24–2	Andy Baylock	6th place
1974	17–22–3	Andy Baylock	6th place
1975	26–16	Jack Gillis	1st—lost in championship
1976	13–27–1	Jack Gillis	7th place
1977	5–16–1*	Dan Gooley	—
1978	18–24	Steve Steitz	7th place
1979	18–23	Andy Baylock	5th place
1980	26–15–1	Al Worthington	2nd place—won title
1981	17–25	Jack Leggett	7th place
1982	14–25–1	Jeff Albies	8th place
1983	11–29–1	Bob Alietta	8th place
1984	20–19–3	Ed Lyons	5th place
1985	13–29	Jim Frye	8th place
1986	19–20–2	Ed Cardieri	5th place
1987	11–30	Ed Cardieri	8th place
1988	18–21	Bill Lagos	4th place, West
1989	18–26	Rich Piergustavo	5th place, West
1990	17–26–1	Dan O'Brien	5th place, West
1991	19–25	Ace Adams	5th place, West
1992	18–23–2	Ace Adams	4th place, West
1993	22–21	Ace Adams	4th place, West
1994	26–16–1	Harvey Shapiro	1st in West—lost in playoffs
1995	16–26–1	Harvey Shapiro	4th place, West
1996	26–17–0	Harvey Shapiro	2nd in West—lost in playoffs
1997	24–20–0	Harvey Shapiro	3rd place, West

* Discontinued operations on July 15, 1977

Player Records

Batting Average: (aluminium bats)	Sam Nattile	1981	.443
Home Runs:	Jim McCollom	1984	15
Runs Batted In:	Doug Fisher	1984	54
Stolen Bases:	Tony Blackmon	1986	17
ERA:	Sam Militello	1989	1.03
Wins:	Bobby St. Pierre	1994	9
Strikeouts:	St. Pierre	1994	72
Saves:	Scott Winchester	1994	13

Falmouth's current home, Fuller Field, is named after Elmer Fuller, who quarterbacked Lawrence High in 1905 and 1906, and scored the game-winning touchdown in the annual Hyannis-Lawrence matchup in 1905. Fuller went on to coach the Falmouth High football team from 1926 through 1946, compiling a 96–55–20 record, winning five Cape championships, and posting three undefeated seasons. He was the athletic director until his retirement in 1952, when the field was named in his honor. He died in 1981 at the age of 93. Recalls Al Irish, who worked with Fuller as the manager of several high school teams in the '30s:

"I was manager of the football team in '36, and assistant manager of the basketball team in 1937, so I worked under Guv Fuller and got to know him well. He was a wonderful coach and wonderful person, and he lived to a ripe old age. He had tennis courts down at Falmouth Heights, and I remember him out playing tennis when he was in his early nineties."

In the early days of the 20th century, the real baseball talent wasn't on the Falmouth town team, but on several of the other semipro teams in town.

"There was a Falmouth town team, but it didn't amount to much," said Tod Owen, who played in Falmouth from 1907 through 1911. "That is to say, most of the players on the Cottage Club, a local semipro team, were most all college players, maybe just freshmen and sophomores, and perhaps more talented than the town team."

And famous Cape Codders recognized that as well. According to Owen, the Cottage Club had connections with a famous relative of the the Kennedy family.

Falmouth's Guv Fuller Field was named after the legendary
Falmouth High football coach in 1952 after he retired. The
field, which also serves at the home of the FHS football
team in the fall, has played host to the Commodores
for many years, and continues to serve as
their home field today.
Photo by Brenda Sharp/courtesy of
Falmouth Historical Society.

"The last couple of years I was there, our team was sponsored by Honey Fitz, the Mayor of Boston," Owen said. "He had a good Irish tenor and would always sing 'Sweet Adeline.' And he supplied our uniforms."

In the early days of the league, the Falmouth town team played on the Central Park grounds. They later moved on to Falmouth Heights, recalled as one of the most beautiful ballparks on the East Coast. Sitting right on the ocean, it was constantly filled with Falmouth supporters, rooting for top-notch talent like future Hall of Famer Pie Traynor.

A native of Framingham, Massachusetts, Traynor played shortstop for the Falmouth town team in 1919. That year, he was one of the league's best hitters, and displayed his all-around skill in the Falmouth Labor Day field events. He won the "circling the bases" event in a time of 15 seconds, the 100-yard dash (in just over 10 seconds), and the "throwing the ball for distance" competition.

The 19-year old was also turning in performances good enough to be noticed by the local press. After going 2 for 4 with a double the previous day, the August 30th issue of the *Falmouth Enterprise* remarked: "The playing of Trainor (*sic*) and the pitching of Carney were the features" in the Falmouth victory. Box scores from that season indicate that Traynor spent most of the season hitting cleanup, and playing shortstop for the Falmouth team.

Traynor would spend 17 years with the Pirates, posting a career batting average of .320 with 1,273 RBI. However, many feel that since his appearance pre-dated the beginning of the organized league—1923—he should not be named as one of the league's former members. While the league officers include him in much of their public relations literature, many skeptics still shake their heads.

"Falmouth Heights—that was a great place to watch a game," recalls Irish, who saw his first game there in 1925. "In those days, there weren't so many other things to do. People went to the ballgame, especially on weekends. It was really crowded, along the banks and the baselines. And you could look out over the water and enjoy the nice ocean breeze."

The only problem, according to Irish, was the short right field, guarded by a house that occasionally made things difficult.

"If it hit the house, it was a double," said Irish. "They had screening set up on the house to protect it in case anything hit it, but some batters could still knock one over the screen."

The 1929 team could have been one of the most star-crossed in the long history of Falmouth baseball. The season began with high hopes, a new manager, and plenty of promise. Everett Donaghey, who captained the 1929 Harvard team, was selected to lead the Falmouth team back to their accustomed spot near the top of the Cape League standings. However, things got off to a rocky start, and Falmouth soon found itself in last place in the five-team league. But a quick change of managers soon changed their luck.

Whereas the 1988 Boston Red Sox used a dose of "Morgan Magic" in winning 12 straight and 19 of 20 to vault them into the driver's seat on the way to the American League East title, the 1929 Falmouth club used what might have been called "Falmouth Fantasy." Starting with a 4–1 exhibition win over the House of David, they won nine straight and 12 of their next 13 to jump from last to first in just a two-week span. However, reality soon prevailed and they fell out of the pennant race.

But the players had become so beloved as a team during their streak fans at the final contest against Hyannis collected money toward the purchase of tiny, golden charm baseballs for team members as a reward for a job well done during the 1929 campaign.

Falmouth was also the first team to have night games on a fairly regular basis, although the early efforts under the lights were greeted with mixed results. In the first non-exhibition tilt under the lights (an exhibition took place approximately a year before) Falmouth met Barnstable under portable lights on July 19, 1939, four years after the majors saw their first night game. For the disgruntled players as well as the estimated 1,200 people who attended (643 paid admissions), the lights were said to have provided subpar illumination. It was reported that shadows and darkness caused baseballs to be dropped and even lost. When the Barnstable scorer asked Falmouth manager Pete Herman how to record a drive knocked down by an infielder but lost in the

Two different views of what many considered the finest Cape
ballpark of the early 20th century, Falmouth Heights. The
proximity to the ocean kept fans cool on hot summer
afternoons, and the land between the sea and the
field allowed fans enough room to park their cars.
(If the batter hit the porch on the house beyond the right-
centerfield fence, it was ruled a ground-rule double.)
Photos courtesy of the Falmouth Historical Society.

Cottage Club 1; Sandwich 0; Falmouth Heights, Aug. 9, 1913.

shadows, Herman replied, "Make note of the fact that he got through the play alive."

One of the more recognizable names to come through the league in the late '60s and early '70s was Steve Greenberg, the son of the famous Tigers slugger. Greenberg was notable for his power, as demonstrated by the manner in which he greeted former Falmouth pitcher Mike Rainnie on his first day in a Falmouth uniform.

"It was my first day out there and I was the first batting practice pitcher," Rainnie said. "Hank Greenberg's son was the first man up, and he hit my first two pitches over the road beyond the left field fence, about 430 feet. Manager Bill Livesey came over to me and said 'Welcome to the Cape League, son.'"

"A guy that I thought would go far was Steve Greenberg," said former umpire Curly Clement. "He played in Falmouth for three years and went to Yale. A smart guy who could have probably played pro ball, he wanted an education instead. He also worked under Fay Vincent when Vincent was the commissioner of baseball." Greenberg is currently the president of the Classic Sports Network.

During the modern era, the Falmouth heyday came in the late '60s and early '70s. Just as Cotuit had dominated in the early '60s with four straight titles, the Commodores took four straight championships from 1968 to 1971, and, as a result of some memorable playoff matchups, initiated a fierce rivalry with the Orleans Cardinals and the Chatham A's in the late '60s and early '70s.

But the hard-charging Commodores always took their cue from Livesey.

"Bill Livesey *was* baseball to me," said Mike Rainnie, who played with Falmouth from 1969 through 1971. "He taught me everything I know about baseball, and I'm still coaching the game 25 years later. I didn't play much for him, but I learned everything I know now from Livesey. First and third situations, pitching and catching, all that strategy there. He was just a very good teacher when it came to the game of baseball."

Former league PR official Dick Bresciani remembers the battles of the late '60s and early '70s between Bill Livesey, Orleans' Tony Williams, and Chatham's Joe Lewis, Jr.

"There was a keen sense of competition between Bill Livesey, Tony Williams, and Joe Lewis, Jr. And it could get pretty heated. Those three guys would bring in good players all the time, and they had some great games.

"There was a tremendous playoff series in '69 between Orleans and Chatham. Falmouth had won their series against Cotuit. And if you look back at that season, there were two or three ties between Falmouth and Orleans. And it was just an exciting thing.

"I remember Orleans, in their final game, at Chatham, had a two run lead in the bottom of the ninth, with two outs and nobody on base. It was reminiscent of the Red Sox in 1986, in Game 6 [of the World Series]. Only this was the *final* game. And Joe Antorino, a righthander from the University of Maryland was throwing for Falmouth. Chatham rallied, scored three runs and won the game, in the dusk and long shadows."

But perhaps the series that had the most fireworks took place in 1971, when Falmouth faced Orleans in a best-of-five championship series. It would be some of the finest baseball the the league had ever seen, and perhaps the most memorable series in CCBL history. The two teams split magnificently pitched 1–0 games at the start of the series, and Falmouth took game three by a 3–1 score. It was in this game that the bad blood started. Falmouth first baseman Brian Herosian collided with Orleans's Brian Martin as Martin slid back to first on an attempted pickoff play. Martin suffered a shoulder injury, and was out for the rest of the playoffs. The Cardinals didn't forget, and neither did Herosian.

Herosian was legendary for his toughness. A former Falmouth teammate remembers that when Herosian came down with a case of poison ivy that summer, he simply scratched it until it was bloody, and then poured gasoline on the open wounds so that they would heal faster.

The fourth game was set for Sunday afternoon in Orleans. The Cardinals led 2–1 entering the top of the sixth. Falmouth's Herosian led off with a walk, and took off for second on the first pitch. He was tagged hard by shortstop Bob Austin, and called out. After getting up, Herosian charged Austin. Both dugouts quickly emptied, and there were fist fights all around the infield. During the fracas, Herosian apparently punched second base umpire and former Cape League pitcher Cal Burlingame. Pitcher Mike Rainnie remembers:

"David Creighton, one of our bench jockeys and local guys, he went after the pitcher. Our catcher, Charlie Hohl, went and got their catcher. I went after the first baseman."

After the umpires had restored order, Herosian, Creighton, and Hohl were ejected. As they walked down the left field line towards the vistors' parking lot, they were showered with boos and taunts from the Orleans crowd on the other side of the field.

"So Brian Herosian's father comes running out from the Falmouth stands by the third base side, and high-tails it to the Orleans side," Rainiee remembers. "All he's got on is a pair of Bermuda shorts — that's it. No shoes, shirt or anything. And he's standing there and pointing at the Orleans stands, and he's calling them every name in the book. Then, when somebody says something back at him, he jumps right up into the stands, pushing old ladies out of the way, and clawing after the guy who said this.

"In all the commotion, Herosian is now in left field, and he turns around and sees his father up in the Orleans stands, so all three of the guys that got tossed start running towards the first base line. And when we see them going, we all come out from our dugout again."

In the ensuing chaos, a young woman and a seven-year-old girl were dragged into the fight, with the young woman receiving a slight concussion. And after 15 minutes of what the *Cape Codder* would call "utter insanity," the Orleans police were called in to quell the riot. Charges were brought against both Herosians.

"It was a pitched battle," recalled Rainnie. "We were dragging back the wounded, and the whole place was just chaos. The guy was on the loudspeaker, trying to calm everybody down. And then two police cruisers pulled up with lights flashing."

The Orleans crowd wanted to press charges against them immediately, but cooler heads eventually prevailed and the game continued. Things proceeded without incident for the next two innings, until the bottom of the eighth inning, when Falmouth manager Bill Livesey was ejected by umpire John McGinn and had to be escorted from the field by an Orleans police officer. Orleans scored three runs in the bottom of the eighth and held on for the 7–5 win. The series was sent back to Falmouth for the fifth and deciding game.

Bob Lukas of Falmouth and Tom White of Orleans matched zeroes through six innings. White, who had shut out Falmouth 1–0 in Game One, began to tire in the seventh. Falmouth's Dave Creighton walked and stole second. Ray O'Brien singled to left, and was waved home by the third base coach.

Orleans outfielder Brian Linden threw home, but it was too high. Creighton slid under the tag, and Falmouth had a 1–0 lead. The Commodores held on through the eighth and ninth, and finally won this bitterly contested series. Because three games ended with a 1–0 score, many felt that this may have been the greatest championship and most bitterly contested series the Cape League had ever seen. Players from that era attribute the Commodores' success to an excellent team chemistry.

"We just had a great group of kids," said Mike Rainnie. "I've been in and out of the Cape League for years since then, coaching, and even throwing batting practice. I don't see the kind of camaraderie now that we had in those days. We were a very tight-knit group of kids, which was very unusual. In the Cape League, guys come from all over the country and are just thrown together. But for some reason, our teams really jelled."

One team that didn't get a chance to enjoy such camaraderie was the 1977 Falmouth club, one of the most unique in the league's modern history. The 1977 Falmouth season started optimistically enough. There was an energetic, young manager, the 30-year-old Dan Gooley, and 17 of the 18 players on the pre-season roster were new. Included among them was a 19-year-old second baseman and future major leaguer from Miami of Ohio named Billy Doran. The Falmouth organization was trying to eliminate all the negativity that surrounded the 1976 team, and their very un-Falmouth like record of 13–27–2. Gooley told the *Falmouth Enterprise* in a season preview: "We're the new kids on the block with a new coach and a new attitude. We're going to re-establish a winning attitude in this town."

However, the club started 2–9, and were only marginally better than the second-year expansion franchise in Hyannis. But at the end of the month of June, Gooley and the rest of the team were confident that they could turn around their sagging fortunes. After all, they had lost six games by one run, and lost four games after taking a lead in the eighth inning.

But July would turn out to be the cruelest month for the Commodores. On July 9, four valuable Commodores were involved in a car crash. Outfielder Tom Grant (blood clot in spleen), third baseman Dave Showalter (broken nose), along with pitchers David Flanagan (stitches to close a facial laceration) and Bill Shortell (facial lacerations and a wrenched knee) were all hospitalized. Later that week, they dropped a 21–9 decision to Hyannis, in a game that was so out of reach that starting second baseman Doran put in a relief appearance.

And the season would get worse. Soon after, catcher Fred Pusterino had three cups of hot coffee accidentally poured down his back in a local restaurant, and Doran suffered a wrist injury after being hit by a pitch.

And jobs had become an issue as well. In the July 15, 1977 issue of the *Falmouth Enterprise*, Gooley confided that he was "extremely concerned" that many of the players were unhappy at their jobs.

"One player still does not have a job, and some others are working only part-time, trying to make ends meet; out of a roster of 19 players, only 13 are active, and finally, some players are not happy with where they are living," said the story.

To remedy the situation, Gooley was scheduled to meet with the Falmouth Chamber of Commerce later that week. "We need help," Gooley added.

But the day before Gooley was to meet with the Falmouth Chamber of Commerce, the players surprised him with an announcement. The night before, they had voted.

Catcher Mark Chicoine told the *Enterprise* on July 22 that the matter came down to money. "None of us are happy," he said. "Nobody wanted to quit . . . everybody wanted to play." He added that none of the players expected to save money over the summer, but each wanted to make enough money for rent and to "have a meal on the table every night."

In recent years, the most famous member of the Commodore braintrust may have been 1983 field manager Bob Alietta. He played in the Cape League with the Commodores for some time before moving on to the majors, but his greatest achievement came when, as a journeyman catcher with the California Angels, he caught one of Nolan Ryan's seven no-hitters.

Harwich native Fred Ebbett (left), seen here at the 1993 All-Star Game, presided over some of the most dramatic moves in league history in his 14-year tenure as league commissioner. He oversaw the Cape League's decision to become a wood bat league, as well as the decision to ban smokeless tobacco.
Photo courtesy of Judy Scarafile.

Harwich Mariners

"I had a great time when I was with Harwich. We had a real good team, and it was probably the best time I had ever had playing ball. It was a great experience for me. We won the championship, and that was the only team that I have ever been on that won the whole thing. So that was a lot of fun."

— Bob Hamelin, 1987 Harwich Mariners

CCBL Members: 1927 (shared franchise with Chatham), 1930–39, 1947–Present
CCBL Championships: 1933, 1983, 1987
Noted Major League Alumni: Joe Magrane ('84), Hal Morris, Paul Sorrento, Todd Stottlemyre ('85), Charles Nagy, Bob Hamelin, Gary DiSarcina ('87)
Field Location: Whitehouse Field, Oak Street, Harwich Center. Follow the signs for Whitehouse Field at the blinking light on Route 124 and Queen Anne Road to the third right on Oak Street. Travel past Cranberry Valley Golf Course on the left, a working cranberry bog on the right, and take a left into the parking lot of the Harwich Public School Administration building.

Oak Street also runs directly into Harwich center for those traveling from the south.

The Mariners play all their home games at 7 P.M. The field is completely fenced in and has elevated bleachers between home plate and each dugout. There is some room for spectators behind the backstop at home plate, but fans there will often be elbow-to-elbow with major league scouts who set up their lawn chairs, radar guns and notebooks while looking for the next star. Today, Whitehouse Field is the most symmetrical ballpark in the Cape League. It's 330 feet down the lines and 400 feet to dead center.

(Incidentally, the freshly-baked cookies prepared in the lower-level of the press box are the best in the league.)

Team records

		Manager	Finish
1965	10–23	n/a	7th place
1966	18–16	n/a	4th place
1967	13–26	n/a	5th place
1968	26–13	n/a	4th place
1969	18–25	John Carroll	6th place
1970	11–28	Don Stanford	4th place
1971	11–30–1	Fred Ebbett	8th place
1972	16–25–1	Fred Ebbett	5th place
1973	15–25–2	George Woodworth	7th place
1974	21–20–1	George Woodworth	3rd place — lost in playoffs
1975	15–25–2	Fred Ebbett	7th place
1976	20–22	Fred Ebbett	5th place
1977	18–22–1	Fred Ebbett	5th place
1978	20–20–2	Don Prohovich	3rd place — lost in playoffs
1979	21–20	Don Prohovich	3rd place — lost in champ.
1980	14–27–1	Don Prohovich	7th place
1981	23–17–2	Don Prohovich	2nd place — lost in playoffs
1982	17–24	Don Prohovich	7th place
1983	24–17–1	Steve Ring	3rd place — lost in playoffs
1984	27–15	Steve Ring	1st place — lost in playoffs

		Manager	**Finish**
1985	22–18–2	Steve Ring	3rd place — lost in playoffs
1986	18–24	Steve Ring	6th place
1987	26–15	Bill Springman	1st place — won championship
1988	21–22	Mike Kinnersley	3rd in East
1989	19–24–1	Mike Kinnersley	4th in East
1990	22–21–1	Fran O'Brien	4th in East
1991	11–33	Steve Ring	5th in East
1992	20–23–1	Steve Ring	3rd in East
1993	11–31–1	Jay Kemble	5th in East
1994	16–25–2	Bruce Peddie	5th in East
1995	15–27–1	Jay Kemble	5th in East
1996	20–22–2	Mike Maack	3rd in East
1997	22–22–0	Chad Holbrook	1st in East — lost in champ.

Player Records

Batting Average:	Rod Peters	1981	.409
(wooden bats):	Scott Hemond	1986	.358
Home Runs:	Cory Snyder	1982	22
Runs Batted In:	Snyder	1982	50
Stolen Bases:	Abbey Gladstone	1976	29
ERA:	Terry Harvey	1992	1.03
Wins:	Oz Griebel	1970	8
	Santerre	1968	8
	Jacobs	1968	8
Saves:	Brian Meyer	1985	6

Prior to moving into Whitehouse Field in 1969, Harwich played their games at Brooks Park. They had never fielded a particularly competitive club, but always managed to have more fun than most clubs. The teams of the ´20s were legendary, and there were many strange stories surrounding Harwich baseball.

For example, a man on a motorcycle turned up one night, carrying with him only a few bats and a knapsack. He demanded to see manager Neil Mahoney, who would later go on to become Farm Director of the Red Sox. Saying only that he was "forty-something," he was penciled into the starting lineup a few days later after an impressive tryout and one of the starters went down with an injury. He got three hits that night, rapped out two more the next afternoon, and the baseball fans of Harwich were delirious with joy. They had found their next star.

But just as quickly as he came, the mystery man vanished the next day. He had been paid a week in advance, and was never heard from again.

In the '40s and '50s, there was a fierce rivalry between Harwich and Chatham. Wally Raneo, who was a catcher for Harwich and the Cape Verdean teams in the late '40s and early '50s, recalls the battles between the town teams: "There would be close to 2,000 people every time we played Chatham in the '50s. A lot of times, you couldn't find a place to park."

The Harwich team soon established a permanent home at Brooks Park, near Harwich High School. Brooks Park had a deep left field, with a house far off in the distance. Reportedly, George Colbert, longtime fan favorite and catcher for both Barnstable and Chatham, was the only player to have ever hit the house on the fly. However, Colbert would later dispute this with his trademark self-deprecating humor. Former Harwich High athletic director Charlie Dunbar explained to the *Cape Cod Times* on the occasion of Colbert's death:

"I was introducing him at a sports banquet and I referred to a home run he once hit in a Cape League game at Brooks Park in Harwich," recalled Dunbar. "Supposedly, he was the only one to have hit a ball off the roof of the house in left field. Well, when he came up to speak he said he couldn't have hit that house if he used a cannon. That's the type of guy he was."

While Harwich hasn't always been the most competitive team, they have always given their fans an entertaining summer. The 1968 season didn't promise to be much better than the 1967 season for the Mariners, but at least long-suffering Mariner fans had the promise of a new ballpark to look forward to in 1969. Manager John Carroll, who also worked as the baseball coach at Natick High, led a team full of local players, from Boston College's Peter Ford (a graduate of Harwich High) to many other players from Tufts, Lynn English High, and other points throughout eastern Massachusetts.

But the 1968 Mariners gave old Brooks Park the best going-away present they could think of, spending the majority of the season at or near the top of the Lower Cape Division. They thrilled their fans by making it into the championship series against perennial powerhouse Falmouth, and raised spirits even higher after taking the first contest from the Commodores. It was played at Brooks Park.

However, the clock had struck twelve for the Cinderellas from Harwich. It would be the last game played at Brooks, as the Commodores quickly ended the series with three straight wins at Falmouth.

Named after Mr. B.F.C. Whitehouse, Whitehouse Field was dedicated in July of 1969 in conjunction with the town's 275th anniversary. It quickly gained a reputation as a pitcher's park, with league commissioner Bernie Kilroy (himself a fair pitcher for Cotuit during their glory days in the 1960s) noting at the park's dedication that the outfield fences looked so far away, "I wish that I was one of the starting pitchers tonight."

Deputy commissioner Robert McNeece of Chatham followed by saying that he hoped the new park would bring many wins to the Harwich club. "Except, of course, when they play Chatham." Finally, Mr. Whitehouse spoke, saying that he hoped that the new field would serve as a great place to play for Harwich, as well as the rest of the league. He ended on a dramatic note, pointing to the Harwich bench and exhorting them to "Now go out and beat Chatham!"

The 1981 season was an interesting one for Harwich. The Mariners were playing well, and they also had Mike Yastremzski on their roster. Son of the Red Sox legend Carl, the Florida State product was a pretty fair college player in his own right, handling first base and the outfield with ease.

When the major league baseball strike began that summer, father Carl found himself with free time on his hands. In late June, he began attending Mariner contests to see his son, who was having a fine year at the plate. Unfortunately, the fans who were attending Mariner games recognized Yaz, and he quickly became the center of attention, regardless of what might have been transpiring on the field of play. Eventually, the problem was solved by having Yastremzski sit in the dugout during games, where he offered batting tips to some of the Mariner players, much to the chagrin of manager Don Prohovich.

The Mariners held first place through much of the month of June and their spirited play, along with the occasional presence of a future Hall-of-Famer had them drawing crowds of over 2,000 to their little woodland ballpark in Harwich.

And as the CCBL moved past the rest of the other summer college circuits in 1985 with the move to wood, Harwich natives will never let you forget it was with a Harwich man at the helm. Harwich's Fred Ebbett assumed the role of league commissioner in 1984, and he would help guide the league through perhaps their most momentous stretch, overseeing the move to wooden bats a year later, as well as the decision to make the CCBL a tobacco-free league in 1993.

Ebbett arrived on the Cape in 1959, when he began teaching business at Harwich High. He started coaching the high school baseball team in 1961, and would go on to lead them to 15 league championships in 21 years. His association with the Cape League began in 1970, when he assumed the role of manager of the Harwich franchise through the 1975 campaign. Fourteen years later, he rose through the ranks to become league commissioner. He retired before the 1997 season.

Whitehouse Field also saw the season opener of the 1988 season, with Thomas P. "Tip" O'Neill in attendance. The former Speaker of the U.S. House of Representatives threw out the first ball, and presented the Mariners with their 1987 championship trophy under a brand-new $38,000 lighting system.

Hyannis Mets

"As I have moved forward in my baseball career, I have become more and more appreciative of the experience on Cape Cod in my development as a player and as a person. It is clearly one of the best, if not the best, amateur leagues in the country."

— Nat "Buck" Showalter, 1976 Hyannis Mets

CCBL Members: 1923–30, 1976–Present
CCBL Championships: 1926,* 1927, 1978, 1979, 1991
(* denotes 1926 championship shared with Osterville)
Noted Major League Alumni: Albert Belle ('87), Robin Ventura ('87), John Valentin, Jeromy Burnitz ('88), Tyler Greene ('89), Brent Gates ('91), Matt Morris ('93)
Field Location: McKeon Field, High School Road, Hyannis. A park with a beautiful view of the Hyannis Inner Harbor beyond the right field fence, McKeon Field is located on High School Road, two blocks south of Main Street behind the old Barnstable High School.

The slope along the left field line may be too steep for lawn chairs, but it is ideal for a blanket full of fans. There are sets of small bleachers located along the first and third base lines for those who prefer to be closer to the action.

Team Records

		Manager	Finish
1976	21–20–1	Ben Hays	4th place, lost in playoffs
1977	15–21–4	Ben Hays	7th place
1978	31–11	Bob Schaefer	1st place, won championship

191

		Manager	**Finish**
1979	33–7–1	Bob Schaefer	1st place, won championship
1980	18–23–1	Rich Magner	6th place
1981	20–22	Rich Magner	5th place
1982	22–19–1	Rich Magner	3rd place, lost in playoffs
1983	20–17–4	Rich Magner	4th place, lost in playoffs
1984	16–25–1	Rich Magner	7th place
1985	17–24–1	Rich Magner	6th place
1986	17–24–1	Frank Cacciatore	7th place
1987	25–16	Dave Holliday	3rd, lost in playoffs
1988	26–17	Wayne Graham	2nd, West – lost in playoffs
1989	24–20	Ed Lyons	2nd, West – lost in championship
1990	20–23–1	Brad Kelley	3rd in West
1991	26–16–2	Brad Kelley	2nd, West – lost in championship
1992	17–26	Glenn Tufts	5th in West
1993	25–19	Steve Mrowka	2nd in West, lost in playoffs
1994	21–21–1	Steve Mrowka	3rd in West
1995	22–20–1	Steve Mrowka	3rd in West
1996	20–24	Steve Mrowka	4th in West
1997	19–23–2	Steve Mrowka	5th in West

Player Records

Batting Average:	Nat "Buck" Showalter	1976	.434
Home Runs:	Bill Schroeder	1978	15
(wood bats)	Joe Vitiello	1990	10
Runs Batted In:	Chris Morgan	1983	51
Stolen Bases:	Corey Zawadsky	1981	17
ERA:	Jim Bisceglia	1985	1.09
Wins:	Pat Hope	1987	11
Strikeouts:	Pat Hope	1987	96
Saves:	n/a		

Barnstable's seven villages have always played an integral role in baseball's development in southeastern Massachusetts. Prior to the arrival of the Hyannis Mets in the mid-'70s, baseball had been played in the Hyannis area as early as the middle of the 19th century. Teams from Osterville, Hyannis and Barnstable all competed at one time or another in the league. The Barnstable villages of Cotuit and Hyannis both have teams in the Cape League today.

Despite being known as the Barnstable town team, the team (known at one time as the Red Sox) lived and played within the village of Hyannis. The land for the field was donated by Albert Hallet, who was a wealthy man and a baseball fanatic. In return, the team named its ballpark Hallett's Field.

The village of Osterville has a proud baseball history as well. In the '20s, they were fierce rivals with Barnstable, and constantly vied for league supremacy. It was home to "Deacon" Danny MacFayden, who many argue was the greatest Cape Cod native ever to play the game.

Osterville was not only home to MacFayden, but to several other noted players who made their mark on the game. Players such as Shanty Hogan, Haskell Billings (who went on to have a cup of coffee with the Detroit Tigers), Eddie Jerrimia (who would go on to play professional hockey, and later take over as the head coach of the Dartmouth hockey program), and Myles Lane (who would go on to prosecute Alger Hiss) all took the field for Osterville in the early days of the league.

But it has always been a struggle for Hyannis to support a team. This was obvious as far back as 1928, when a report in the *Patriot* took the Hyannis fans to task for not supporting their team. After a close second-place finish to Osterville, the paper viewed the lack of public support as the primary reason for the team's downfall: "Officials of the Hyannis team have said that due to the lack of support by local people the season was anything but a financial success for that team. Public spirited citizens who gave the other teams in the league the proper backing failed to come forward or did not make good their promise of support for the Hyannis team.

Altho the gate receipts were up to the usual average, the heavy expense of operating a team in the league makes financial support from other sources, a necessity."

After baseball left Barnstable in the '40s, there was no league presence in the area until the Hyannis franchise was organized in 1976 to bring the league back up to eight teams after the demise of the Bourne Canalmen. When Hyannis received a franchise in 1976, the team was named the Mets with the hope of receiving some sort of financial assistance from the New York Mets, but it was turned down.

They first played their games on the old Barnstable High field, located behind the school on West Main Street. However, it was clear that they would have to move to larger accommodations. They made the playoffs in their inaugural season, led by Buck Showalter's league-leading .434 mark, and won the league championship in 1978. Their success made it possible to consider the idea of moving their home field to a more permanent site.

McKeon Field took two years to build, and was a long and arduous process. In the '20s, a WPA project had cleared away some of the Hyannis forest near the harbor. The land had been filled in and used as a ballfield during the Depression, but was virtually unplayable in the late '70s. The Mets organization was given permission by the town to renovate the area, providing it cost the town nothing.

Thanks to Jack Aylmer, a former state senator who was named to spearhead the new franchise, thousands of dollars in wire, cable. lights, lamps and other components were donated to the project. Twelve electrical distributors and contractors came in to help with the process. The light towers were donated by area power companies.

"Making the playoffs the first year was a help," Aylmer recalls. "But when we were playing on West Main Street at the time, it was twilight baseball, the crowds were not that good at all compared to veteran franchises like Chatham. So we decided to move downtown, and got everyone in town who owned a dump truck, a back hoe, a front end loader or a bulldozer to chip in and volunteer their time. We got the loam donated, dugouts, press box — the whole bit."

The 1976 edition of the Hyannis Mets included future major league manager Buck Showalter (back row, second from left), who ended up leading the league in hitting that year with a .434 mark and capturing league MVP honors. Showalter is shown below accepting the MVP trophy.
Photos courtesy of Jack Aylmer.

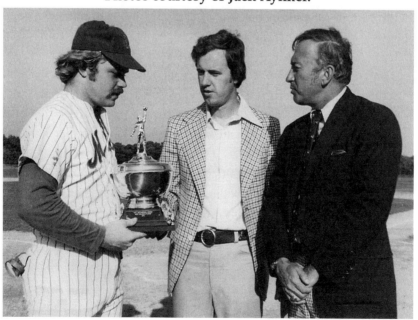

After diverting a stream that ran through the outfield and pushing back the hillside that runs along the third base line, volunteers workers erected the fences, built the dugouts, and laid the playing surface.

Named after the late John McKeon, a local athlete and member of the Barnstable School Committee who contributed mightily to the town's athletic programs, it was inaugurated in the summer of 1979, with the Mets taking their second consecutive Cape League title. Lights were installed in 1983 at a cost of $75,000.

With the only major mall on the Cape, plenty of fast food restaurants, and an airport, Hyannis is the closest thing to a city that the Cape has. This city-like environment is embraced by the tourists and provides rainy-day activity for people throughout the Cape. This is a big plus for Hyannis merchants, but not for the team.

"I hate to say it, but Hyannis is one of the more difficult franchises to keep going," says Aylmer. "By and large, it's a place to work, and not necessarily a place to live. Hyannis loads up with daytime employees who then escape to their villages after work. They don't want to stay in Hyannis to watch baseball. And bear in mind that Cape League baseball is not the only show in town," Aylmer said. "Unlike Orleans, Harwich, Chatham or Brewster. Hyannis offers a wide variety of restaurants, nightclubs, movie theatres, the mall and the Cape Cod Melody Tent. So there are a lot of choices for evening entertainment."

Hyannis manager Steve Mrowka agrees, but adds a twist.

"Hyannis is a lot different than most towns here on the Cape," Mrowka said. "There is a lot to do, more traditional city-type stuff like bars and clubs. Because of that, it's a good town to recruit players. But once we get them here, it's tough to keep them focused."

One of the reasons the Mets were so successful in the late '70s was the decision to hire Bob Schaefer. But when Schaefer was hired, several people active in the Hyannis organization looked down on him. Despite his success at Norwich High in Connecticut, he was still considered only a high school coach. But in one of the nicer stories in Cape League history, Schaefer soon won more than the respect of Hyannis baseball fans.

After winning two consecutive titles, and making the Mets into

Home of the Hyannis Mets since 1976, McKeon Field (right) is
situated on the Hyannis waterfront. Visible in the distance are
the docks for the Hyannis fishing fleet and the ferries that
run hourly to Martha's Vineyard and Nantucket.
Photo courtesy of Jack Aylmer.

instant contenders just two years after their inception, he was hired by the Yankees, and proceeded to win minor league championships at every level. He left soon after realizing that the Yankees had no intention of making him a major league manager. He then took jobs with the Mets, Royals, and eventually, the Red Sox as Director of Field Operations for their Minor League System.

"Bob Schaefer was great to play for," said Tom Cahir, who played under Schaefer in 1971 when they were with the Bourne Canalmen. "He loved the game and understood the game. He worked with us to avoid mental mistakes. He always said the physical errors will come, but avoid the mental mistakes and you'll be okay. He was tough, but he was honest with us. That helped in college. It's not surprising, because of his love of the game, to see what he's achieved today."

According to Jack Aylmer, both Bill Livesey and Schaefer have been responsible for many former Cape Leaguers seeing the light of day at the major league level.

"Both Livesey and Schaefer have been responsible for bringing into the major leagues a number of players, many of whom have never been drafted, but were given tryouts, because of their connection with the Cape League," Aylmer said. "The big publicity has always been that there have been a hundred or so players in the majors with Cape League experience with 20 or so drafted every year. But the real story behind the story is the fact that there are a lot of youngsters who play in the Cape League who, by virtue of even being here, get a look-see, a tryout."

Orleans Cardinals

"Playing for Orleans, in the summer of 1984, was probably the best summer of my life. Playing for the U.S. team the next year was a great experience, but nothing could take back from the memories of the times I had in Orleans."

— Erik Hanson, 1984 Orleans Cardinals

CCBL Members: 1928-38, 1947-Present

CCBL Championships: 1947, 1949, 1950, 1952, 1953, 1955, 1957, 1986, 1993

Noted Major League Alumni: Carlton Fisk ('66), Chris Sabo ('82), Jeff Conine ('86), Frank Thomas ('88), J.T. Snow ('88), Ben McDonald ('89), Nomar Garciaparra ('93).

Field Location: Eldredge Park, Route 28, Orleans. All home games at venerable Eldredge Park start at 7 P.M. The field is located at Eldredge Parkway and Route 28 off exit 12 from Route 6. Parking is available in the lot beyond right field, as well as the nearby Nauset Middle School.

Team Records

		Manager	Finish
1965	19–13	n/a	3rd place
1966	19–15	n/a	3rd place
1967	20–20	n/a	4th place
1968	20–19	n/a	3rd place
1969	28–16	Tony Williams	2nd place
1970	23–16	Tony Williams	3rd place
1971	26–12–4	Tony Williams	2nd place

		Manager	Finish
1972	26–15–1	Tony Williams	3rd place
1973	19–21–2	Tony Williams	5th place
1974	20–15–7	Tom Yankus	2nd place
1975	24–16–2	Tom Yankus	2nd place
1976	18–21–2	Tom Yankus	6th place
1977	13–19–9	Tom Yankus	6th place
1978	20–21–1	Tom Yankus	4th place
1979	16–23–3	Tom Yankus	6th place
1980	12–29–1	Tom Yankus	8th place
1981	22–18–2	Jack Donahue	3rd, lost in championship
1982	18–23–1	Jack Donahue	5th place
1983	16–25–1	Jack Donahue	6th place
1984	23–18–1	John Castleberry	4th, lost in playoffs
1985	21–21	John Castleberry	4th, lost in playoffs
1986	25–15–2	John Castleberry	1st place—won title
1987	21–19	John Castleberry	5th place
1988	22–20	John Castleberry	2nd, East—lost in playoffs
1989	13–30–1	John Castleberry	5th place
1990	24–20	John Castleberry	2nd, East—lost in playoffs
1991	21–21–2	Rolando Casanova	2nd, East—lost in playoffs
1992	13–30–1	Rolando Casanova	5th place, East
1993	23–20–1	Rolando Casanova	2nd, East—won title
1994	27–15–1	Rolando Casanova	1st, East—lost in playoffs
1995	22–21–0	Rolando Casanova	2nd, East—lost in playoffs
1996	20–22–1	Rolando Casanova	4th, East
1997	15–29–0	Don Norris	5th, East

Player Records

Batting Average: (aluminium)	John Awdycki	1965	.407
Home Runs:	Gary Alexander	1986	12

Runs Batted In:	Ken Lisko	1981	41
Stolen Bases:	George Minarsky	1970	25
ERA:	Dan Hale	1984	0.95
Wins:	John Howes	1985	7
Saves:	David Shepard	1994	9

Despite the long tradition of on-field excellence enjoyed by the Orleans Cardinals, many feel the most exciting moment in their long history occurred in 1926.

Built nearly 100 years ago, America's first transatlantic cable station was located just up the road from the new ballfield on Route 28, no more than a long fly ball away from the park. Back in the summer of 1926, Orleans was one of the first places in America to receive telegraphed news from Europe. And according to legend, Orleans was the first place in the United States to get the news that Charles Lindbergh had landed safely in Paris.

After the cable from Europe had been received and translated, the excited clerk ran out of the station and down Route 28, where he knew the largest number of townsfolk would be gathered—at the ball game at Eldredge Park.

The clerk breathlessly commandeered the public-address system (a hand-held megaphone) and relayed the historic news to the crowd—Lindbergh had landed in Paris. The baseball fans of Orleans were among the first Americans to hear of Lindbergh's remarkable achievement.

Orleans dominated the league in the late ´40s and throughout the ´50s, winning Cape League titles in 1950, 1952, 1953, 1955 and 1957. The team's success was thanks in no small part to the collection of college and semipro talent that they assembled. While the rest of the league continued with town players, the Cardinals drew some of the best college talent in Massachusetts. According to one player who was in the league at this time, Orleans had 20 players on their roster, and 19 of them were from colleges or semipro teams.

Since the beginning of organized baseball on Cape Cod, the Orleans team has always played at approximately the same site. But before 1966, home plate at Eldredge Park was located in what is now the left field corner of today's ballpark. The sun would set just beyond the treeline in what was then left-center, blinding the batter during late-afternoon contests.

Efforts to rearrange the field began at the 1966 Orleans Town meeting, where the sum of $10,000 was allotted "for the purpose of rehabilitating the recreational facilities at Eldredge Field." An additional $20,000 was then raised to complete the entire project, including the new music shell (later named the Charles F. Moore Bandstand), new tennis courts, new picnic area, and other recreational facilities provided by the master plan. Home plate was moved to where the right field corner was formerly located, which made things much easier for the hitters. The new park debuted just in time for the 1967 league all-star game, and the contest was much like an opening night on Broadway. With eight colorful new pennants—one for each Cape League team (the result of many nights of work by Orleans seamstresses)—flying from the backstop, Massachusetts Governor John A. Volpe and his wife arrived at the game by helicopter. Accompanying him was Lieutenant Governor Francis W. Sargent and Attorney General Elliot Richardson. Volpe threw out the first ball, and all three officials gave speeches to the large crowd. Unlike most politicians, they stayed to watch the entire game.

They were joined by over 13 major league scouts, including Len Merullo of the Cubs (and former Cape Leaguer), Buzz Bowers from the Dodgers, and Clyde Sukeforth from the Braves (legendary for his discovery of Jackie Robinson).

Before the game, the crowd was treated to an old-timers batting practice. It featured Elmer Darling, who played for the first Orleans town team in 1915, pitching to Laurin Peterson, who played catcher in the early days for the Orleans town club. Despite his age, Peterson hit several line drives into left field.

During the game, pitchers were brought to the mound in a golf cart, causing the *Cape Codder* to later remark that "No bush-league stuff around Eldredge Park, you can bet." The golf cart was a donation from Orleans selectman Charles F. Moore. Moore had much to do with the new Eldredge Park, and later received the honor of having his name given to the Charles F. Moore Bandstand, which sits beyond the right centerfield fence at Eldredge Park.

The 2,000 in attendance saw the Lower Cape All-Stars christen the field with a 9–1 victory. A young catcher from Harwich and the University of New Hampshire named Carlton Fisk (identified as "Cal Fisk" in several game stories) started for the Lower Cape, and caught the first five innings.

Former Boston Celtics CEO Dave Gavitt is just one of several Cape League coaches who have gone on to success in other sports. Gavitt managed at Orleans and Harwich for several years in the early days of the league. Another one of the famous individuals is New Jersey Devils GM Lou Lamoriello, who managed at Yarmouth, Bourne, and Sagamore. In addition, Lamoriello played with Orleans.

As a baseball manager, perhaps Dave Gavitt's most intriguing situation came in 1962 in a game at Orleans. Umpire Curly Clement remembers:

"It was Orleans against D-Y, and the score was tied. The Orleans leftfielder was caught at the plate trying to stretch a triple into a home run, and he was out on a close play. The runner had a fistful of sand in his hand and he threw it on my chest. I threw him out of the game. Gavitt came out real slowly and said to me 'Curly, do you know what you just did?'

"'Yes,' I said. 'I threw your left fielder out of the game.'

"'No Curly, I don't mean that,' Gavitt said. 'You just threw my ninth ballplayer out of the game. I've only got eight ballplayers left on the bench.'

"'Are you sure?' I said.

"'Yes,' Gavitt said.

"'I'm sorry, but the game is over,' I said. 'You forfeit the ballgame to Y-D.'

"Gavitt looked at me and started to laugh."

Between the late '60s and early '70s, the field, as well as the organization, had fallen into disrepair. Former public address announcer Ed Mooney called it "mediocre." In addition, there was no booth behind home plate. There was no fencing down the right field line. There was just one set of tiny bleachers, right behind the

Above: Orleans' Eldredge Park, as seen in the early ´70s. Note the steep, overgrown hill and the sparsely populated bleachers. Photo courtesy of Arnold Mycock. *Below:* The grading of the hill along the first base/right field line in the early ´80s, along with the financial strength of the Orleans Cardinals organization, has made Eldredge Park one of the most popular parks in the league. Photo by Michelle Adams.

plate. There were no distance signs on the fences. And there was an old wooden scoreboard that Mooney said "was always running out of twos and threes."

But all that would soon change. Lights were added for the final three games of the 1979 season, which allowed players to work almost exclusively during the day, and then play at night. This made things easier for the organization when it came to finding players.

It was the winter of 1982 when the Cardinals really started to move "into the 20th century," as Mooney puts it.

Mooney, along with general manager Ken Grinder, field manager Jack Donahue, and some other members of the Cardinals committee gathered on the field on a cold day in February. They wondered what else they could do to the field.

They had erected a booth behind home plate for the announcer, as well as the scoreboard operator and the official scorer. The light towers were fully functional, allowing Orleans to be one of the few franchises to have night games. Distance markers were visible on the outfield fences. What more could they do? They stood on the field in freezing temperatures, wondering to themselves.

Donahue turned to the right field line and gazed at the steep hill that prevented many elderly people from getting closer to the action. Moreover, it was almost impossible to sit on while watching the game without sliding down to the bottom of the hill and into short right field.

"Why don't we do something with that hill?" asked Donahue.

The men looked at each other. They all agreed with the idea, and went inside to celebrate with some hot coffee.

One of the Cardinals committee was in the earth-moving business, and as soon as the ground thawed, they went to work. Later that summer, the terracing was finished, and attendance increased dramatically.

The other additions to the park included new bleachers and real dugouts (before there had been just a pair of benches with canvas covering). Today, the 434-foot fence in centerfield is the deepest in the league. However, the 300-foot fence to left is one of the most shallow in the league, which makes for several broken windshields each year in the parking lot beyond the left field fence.

Wareham's Clem Spillane Field played host to the 1993
All-Star Game. Named after the famed Wareham
football coach, it currently serves at the home of the
Wareham Gatemen. Photo courtesy of Judy Scarafile

Wareham Gatemen

"I think my time in the Cape League really helped me learn more about the game of baseball. I was fortunate to play for a guy in Wareham named Joe Arnold that really knew the game. That really helped." — Mickey Tettleton, 1980 Wareham Gatemen

CCBL Members: 1927–32, 1960–Present

CCBL Championships: 1930, 1976, 1988, 1994, 1997

Noted Major League Alumni: Mickey Tettleton, Bob Tewksbury ('80), Pete Incaviglia ('83), Walt Weiss ('84), Maurice (Mo) Vaughn, Chuck Knoblauch ('88)

Field Location: Clem Spillane Field, Route 6, Wareham Center. Located roughly one mile west of Wareham Center. Spillane Field is adjacent to Wareham High and Wareham Middle School, and is one of two Cape League fields used for high school football as well as baseball.

There is a small parking lot on Route 6 that fills quickly before each game, but there's room to park along the access road that winds back from Route 6 past the Boys & Girls Club to Wareham High. Starting time is 7 P.M.

Team records

		Manager	Finish
1965	4–28	n/a	8th place
1966	11–23	n/a	8th place
1967	12–27	n/a	6th place
1968	18–22	n/a	5th place

		Manager	Finish
1969	18–26	Bill Thurston	7th place
1970	25–16	Ed Lyons	1st tie w/Fal., lost in playoffs
1971	23–17–2	Ed Lyons	2nd place, lost in playoffs
1972	14–26–2	Ed Lyons	8th place
1973	21–19–2	Ed Lyons	3rd place, lost in playoffs
1974	23–14–5	Ed Lyons	1st place, lost in playoffs
1975	18–23–1	Ed Lyons	5th place
1976	21–18–2	Bill Livesey	3rd place, won championship
1977	20–20	Bill Livesey	4th place, lost in playoffs
1978	20–22	Demie Mainieri	5th place
1979	17–25	Jack Gillis	7th place
1980	20–20–2	Joe Arnold	4th place, lost in playoffs
1981	27–13–2	Joe Arnold	1st place, lost in playoffs
1982	29–11–1	Joe Arnold	1st place, lost in playoffs
1983	26–15–3	Joe Arnold	2nd place
1984	22–17–3	Mike Roberts	4th place, lost in playoffs
1985	19–22–1	Mark Scalf	5th place
1986	22–18–2	Stan Meek	3rd place, lost in playoffs
1987	17–25	Bob Pearson	6th place
1988	29–13	Stan Meek	1st place — West — won championship
1989	21–22–1	Jim Fleming	4th place — West
1990	24–19–1	Jim Fleming	1st place — West — lost in playoffs
1991	30–14	Don Reed	1st place — West — lost in playoffs
1992	22–20–1	Don Reed	2nd place — West — lost in playoffs
1993	25–17–2	Don Reed	1st place — West — lost in playoffs
1994	25–17–1	Don Reed	1st place — West — won championship
1995	28–15–1	Don Reed	2nd place — West — lost in championship

| 1996 | 29-15-0 | Don Reed | 1st place — West — lost in playoffs |
| 1997 | 28-16-0 | Don Reed | 1st place — West — won championship |

Player Records

Batting Average:	John Morris	1981	.410
Home Runs:	Steve Newell	1973	11
Runs Batted In:	Mike Lopez	1982	52
Stolen Bases:	Roy Marsh	1993	48
ERA:	Brad Clontz	1991	0.91
Wins:	John Thoden	1988	9-1
Saves:	Brad Clontz	1991	11
Strikeouts:	Bobby Sprowl	1976	100

Clem Spillane Field is named after the great football coach at Wareham High, and doubles as the high school football field in the fall. It is known for having some of the most persistent gnats in the league.

The 1930 season saw Wareham take their first league title, which sent the town into a veritable frenzy. The team was feted at a sumptuous banquet at the Old Colony Inn in Wareham, with the Wareham Chamber of Commerce picking up the tab. At the dinner were U.S. Congressman Charles L. Gifford, Senator D.W. Nicholson, team captain H.L. Colbeth, and league vice-president J. Herbert Shepard. All gave lengthy speeches lauding the performance of the Wareham club, and the entire team was presented with watches commemorating the feat.

But in the eyes of the town fathers, this wasn't enough. The team was featured in a huge victory parade that wound through the streets of Wareham, with the entire town turning out to cheer their heroes. Headed by the town band, the team paraded merrily through the streets with their championship banner for the entire afternoon.

During the mid-1930s, the Wareham Twilight League was popular throughout the Upper Cape. Member teams were the Wareham CD, East Wareham Elks, and Tremont AA, Pappi's Live Wires (later renamed Meadowbrook). Atwood AA (of nearby Carver) came into the league soon after. With the exception of the East Wareham team, all games were played on Wareham's Marion Road Field, where the Wareham Town Hall is now.

During the last few years of the Twilight League, the games were moved to the present high school field, Clem Spillane Field. The Twilight League folded shortly after the start of World War II.

With the rebirth of baseball on Cape Cod after the war, the Cape League established a permanent franchise at Wareham. They were immediately a successful club, winning an Upper Cape Championship in 1957. In 1964, lights were installed at Spillane Field at a cost of $17,500 to the town.

With the move to an all-college circuit in the '60s, the Wareham team was nicknamed the Gatemen because, as one league official put it, "They stand at the gates of Cape Cod." They remained extremely competitive, taking their first league championship in the modern era in 1976. That year, they were supported by the legendary John Decas, and coached by Bill Livesey. Decas headed the club from 1976 through 1983, when John Wylde took over as team president. Wylde remains as president today, and spares no expense in the upkeep and care of Clem Spillane Field, truly the gateway to baseball on Cape Cod.

During the 1983 playoffs there was some controversy involving Wareham and their push for a title. The Gatemen were the runners-up to Cotuit during the regular season, posting a 26–15–3 mark on the season. However, Manager Joe Arnold said that, because of roster losses, he would only have a total of 12 players to open the playoffs, and only two of them were infielders.

General manager John Decas advised league officials in early August that even if his team made the playoffs, they would be unable to field a team in the post season. He asked the league to consider adding the fifth-place finisher for the playoffs.

"I was honest and up front," Decas told the *Cape Cod Times* after the season. "I saw the numbers of available players dwindling, and I passed the situation along to the league on more than one occasion. It made sense to do so because it was in the league's best interest."

Manager Joe Arnold also told league officials he could not get by without four regular infielders. According to Wareham officials, then-league commissioner Archie Allen told them that they would be allowed to add only two players at "any position."

According to many, this was the crucial point that led to the dispute between the Wareham club and the league office.

"The league didn't express itself as clearly as it could have about replacing players," league vice-president Frank Green said later. "And Arnold may have been unclear, but he didn't ask for clarification, and he didn't fill any of the player positions."

As a result, Wareham withdrew from the playoffs on August 8th, one day after the end of the regular season and the day before the first round of the playoffs were set to begin. The league created an ad hoc committee to investigate the situation. It included Green, along with former league commissioner Art Hyland, deputy commissioner Fred Ebbett, Don Tullie of Yarmouth-Dennis, and Skip Finnell of Harwich. The committee unanimously decided to suspend the Wareham franchise for one year.

However, after extensive discussion and debate, the league executive committee decided to amend the decision and limit the suspension to just "the present holders" of the Wareham franchise. The vote in favor of that action was nearly unanimous, according to Green.

"The thinking was the league was not willing to put up with the Wareham franchise being run by its present people, but the league still wanted an eighth team," Green explained.

The suspension included the officers and directors of the Wareham Gatemen, but did not name field manager Joe Arnold. According to the league office, the list included Decas as president, Joe Cafarella as vice-president, Albert Tocci as treasurer, and Shirley Alcott as secretary. The directors of the organization were Cafarella, Claire McWilliams, Ozzie Thieman, and Jim Hubbard. The suspension imposed a fine of $750.

"The Cape League has got a lot of nerve," Decas thundered in a the *Cape Cod Times* article. "You can tell them they're not taking anything away from me because I've already withdrawn my support. I'm the chief cook and bottle washer here, but I've had it. As far as the fine goes, frankly, I'm surprised. I don't think there's any justification for it. I'd like to contest it, but I'm up against a kangaroo court. The deck is stacked against me. The league is trying to look good and make Wareham look bad."

"A lot of people misunderstood John Decas," said John Claffey, who worked with Decas on several occasions in Wareham and Hyannis. "He was very loud, very aggressive, put people back on their heels when he spoke to them. He could be fiery, but he was also a guy that would help you out if you needed it and be understanding."

League vice-president Frank Green told the *Cape Cod Times* that the league would entertain applications from interested communities for the following season, including Wareham. As it turned out, Wareham was reinstated, and picked up play without skipping a beat the next year.

But the franchise suffered some tough times through the mid-'80s. When John Wylde and John Claffey came aboard, they brought with them some money and some impressive players. As a result, baseball in Wareham underwent a renaissance. In 1988, they were one of the best teams in the history of the Cape League. Mo Vaughn, along with Chuck Knoblauch, helped lead the Gatemen to 29 wins in 42 games and the league championship.

"We had a good team," Knoblauch recalled. "Everybody knows Mo Vaughn was on that team, and we had a lot of good players that went on to play in the minor leagues, and a couple of them are still playing. It was fun that summer. We only lost 13 games, and won the whole thing. It was definitely exciting."

Mo Vaughn enjoys a special place in the hearts of many New England baseball fans, but the people of Wareham are quick to tell you they saw him first. Vaughn went 11 for 20 in the 1988 post season, helping Wareham thump the opposition on the way to the title.

"I'll say this," Claffey said. "When we arrived here, Wareham was a dead town as far as baseball was concerned. We had trouble drawing fans.

"Then Maurice arrived on the scene, and our attendance increased. Interest in the team increased. And I put all of that credit right in Mo's hands, because he was the one that did it all. I don't care what anybody says, people off the field can do whatever they want, or try as hard, but people come to see the ballplayers. They don't come to see me, John Wylde, or anybody else. They come to see the players. And in 1988, they came to see Mo Vaughn. He brought the game back to Wareham."

And in the early '90s, Don Reed has been one of the main reasons that the game has kept that level of popularity. He won 200 regular season games through his first eight years as a manager in the Cape League, capturing three championships. There are few managers, in the Cape League or throughout the rest of college baseball, who get more out of their players than Reed.

"I've learned so much baseball from him," said Joe Walsh, his longtime pitching coach who has been with Reed at both Y-D and Wareham. "He's like my mentor. The guy gives everything he's got, his heart and soul. And he expects the same out of other people. I've never seen anybody with a work ethic like that."

He has one of the most impressive managerial resumes in Cape League history. He has coached 30 major league players and 150 professional players. As of 1994, eight of his players have been taken in the first round of the amateur draft. In addition to his work with Wareham and Yarmouth-Dennis, Reed has served as a scout for the San Diego Padres and Pittsburgh Pirates. His two sons have had extended professional careers — Curt Reed has played with San Diego and the White Sox, while Jeff has been the backstop for the San Francisco Giants.

But despite his success, he has yet to be embraced by much of the Cape League because of his hard-line, anything-for-a-win attitude that many feel is out of place in the relatively laid back atmosphere of the CCBL. His rough-and-tumble attitude even got him dismissed from the Yarmouth-Dennis managerial job after winning *back-to-back* titles in 1989 and 1990. But having won titles with Wareham in 1994 and 1997, he joins current Tampa Bay Devil Rays director of scouting Bill Livesey (who won championships with Falmouth and Wareham) in being the only men who have won Cape League titles with two different teams.

"I can never compare them because they're different teams, different places, different times," Reed said soon after the 1994 championship. "But they're all great, you love each one of them. You feel just great about it. The big thing is when you see kids

Above: Many credit Mo Vaughn (who attended Seton Hall University), with helping to revive baseball in the town of Wareham. Vaughn was part of the 1988 Gatemen team that won 29 of 42 regular season games,
Photo courtesy of Jack Aylmer.
Below: Currently the dean of Cape League managers, Don Reed (center) has enjoyed tremendous success with both Wareham and Yarmouth-Dennis, and is one of two men to win a Cape League title with two franchises.
Photo courtesy of Judy Scarafile.

come through when the pressure is on, and you find out what kind of character they have, what they're made out of."

In addition, both Reed and Livesey have had their run-ins with league umpires. Longtime umpire Curly Clement recalls an incident in 1993 where he was able to diffuse Reed's temper.

"He came out to change pitchers. I let him talk for a few minutes before I came out and asked 'Are you making a change?'

"He didn't answer. 'Who's coming in?' I asked again.

"'I'm getting goddamn sick of you umpires screwing me,' Reed told Clement under his breath.

"'Reed,' I said. 'Curly has never screwed you. When I screw you, you'll know about it.'

"'How will I know?'

"'I'll kiss you,' I said. And he started to laugh."

"The Cape League is his life," said Russ Charpentier, who covers the league for the *Cape Cod Times*. "When you talk to some of his players, they'll tell you he isn't as tough as a college coach. He just goes against the summer league grain. But you can't argue with his results."

Longtime manager of both the Yarmouth Indians and the Yarmouth-Dennis Red Sox, Merrill "Red" Wilson (left) recently had the the Y-D ballfield named in his honor. Photo courtesy of Arnold Mycock.

Yarmouth-Dennis Red Sox

"I had a chance to play at Y-D for three weeks, and I was lucky enough to get signed. So it was a great move for me, to come to the Cape and get noticed." — Mike Bordick, 1986 Y-D Red Sox

CCBL Members: 1949–Present. From 1949 to the 1960s, Yarmouth and Dennis operated separately. In 1977, the Yarmouth franchise added Dennis, and were known as Y-D.

CCBL Championships: 1958, 1960 (as the Yarmouth Indians), 1989, 1990 (as the Yarmouth-Dennis Red Sox)

Noted Major League Alumni: Steve Balboni ('77), Mike LaValliere ('81), Mike Bordick ('86), Craig Biggio, Mickey Morandini, ('87), Dennis Neagle ('88), Alan Benes ('91)

Field Location: Station Avenue, South Yarmouth. Station Avenue is located off exit 8 on the Mid-Cape Highway. The ballpark is located approximately two miles on the left, behind D-Y High School.

Low bleachers extend along the first and third baselines, and the flat surroundings make it easy to set up a lawnchair and enjoy the action. Parking is no problem, as the big lot behind D-Y Regional High School and the proximity to Route 28 makes pre- and post-game egress easy.

Team Records

		Manager	Finish
1965	16–18	n/a	5th place
1966	12–22	n/a	7th place

		Manager	Finish
1967	20–20	n/a	4th place
1968	16–24	n/a	7th place
1969	21–22	Merrill Wilson	4th place
1970	13–26	Merrill Wilson	6th place
1971	15–23–3	Merrill Wilson	6th place
1972	15–24–3	Merrill Wilson	6th place
1973	19–20–3	Merrill Wilson	4th place, lost in playoffs
1974	16–23–3	Merrill Wilson	7th place
1975	20–20–2	Bob Stead	4th place, lost in playoffs
1976	10–27–4	Bob Stead	8th place
*1977	21–17–3	Bob Stead	3rd place, lost in playoffs
1978	13–29	Brian Sabean, Bob Stead	8th place
1979	14–25–2	Merrill Wilson	8th place
1980	19–21–1	Merrill Wilson	5th place
1981	19–22–1	Merrill Wilson	6th place
1982	18–23–1	Merrill Wilson	5th place
1983	18–18–5	Merrill Wilson	5th place
1984	13-28–1	Merrill Wilson	8th place
1985	14–27–1	Merrill Wilson	7th place
1986	15–23–3	Merrill Wilson	8th place
1987	24–15	Don Reed	2nd — lost in championship
1988	22–18	Don Reed	1st, East — lost in playoffs
1989	28–15–1	Don Reed	1st, East — won title
1990	24–16–3	Don Reed	1st, East — won title
1991	20–22–2	John Barlowe	4th place, East
1992	18–24–1	John Barlowe	4th place, East
1993	22–20–2	John Barlowe	4th place, East
1994	20–21–2	John Barlowe	3rd place, East

1995	17–24–2	John Barlowe	3rd place, East
1996	13–29–2	John Barlowe	5th place, East
1997	19–25–0	Steve Cohen	4th place, East

* Merger between Yarmouth and Dennis

Player Records

Batting Average (aluminium):	Dan Whitworth	1969	.411
(wooden bats):	Jon Petke	1994	.379
Home Runs:	Mark Angelo	1981	14
Runs Batted In:	Mark Angelo	1981	47
Stolen Bases:	Mickey Morandini	1987	43
ERA:	Brad Stuart	1989	1.03
Wins:	Chris Granata	1992	8
	Dave Schuler	1973	8
Saves:	Chris Clemons	1993	10

Yarmouth and Dennis played at several places when they were separate teams, but once they merged, they settled at the Dennis-Yarmouth High School field. They named the field after Merrill "Red" Wilson, the longtime D-Y coach who was part of the Cape League for many years.

In 1996, Wilson was selected to throw out the first ball at the Cape League All-Star Game. The longtime Y-D coach reflected on the tribute soon after.

"Naming the field after me was a great honor," Wilson recalled. "Anyone who has been in sports will tell you that there's no greater way of being remembered. And it came as a complete surprise."

In the late '40s when Dennis played as the Dennis Clippers, their home games were held at Ezra Baker Field in South Dennis. It was considered one of the leading facilities in the league, so much so that the D-Y *Register* noted in 1949: "Practically everything needed for complete enjoyment of a ball game is now offered the fans at the Dennis park."

Merrill Wilson recalled how Baker Field was one of the first to have lights, allowing for the novelty of night baseball. However, everything didn't always work as well as it should have.

"Everyone in the league was excited to play under the lights," Wilson said. "But the only people who really benefited from the lights were the pitcher, catcher and the batter. It became an adventure for the fielders. Usually, when you see a ball go into the air, you'll hear 'I got it.' At Dennis during night games, the usual cry was 'Where is it?'"

In addition to the lights, the 2,500 spectators at the park could follow the game more easily with the new electronic scoreboard, raised six feet so that the entire field could see.

The National Hockey League's New Jersey Devils GM Lou Lamoriello was a part of the Yarmouth organization throughout the '60s, and his Cape baseball legacy is described by former league PR chief Dick Bresciani.

"The year 1967 was the last season that high school players were allowed in the league, and Lamoriello was in Yarmouth. He was an aggressive baseball guy, and he brought in a young centerfielder from Connecticut named Bobby Valentine, who was going into his senior year in high school. The kid struggled for the first month. He wasn't playing well, but he stayed in the lineup because it was clear that he could run and catch the ball. Then he really started to develop, and by the end of the year he was holding his own. Of course, we know what happened to Bobby Valentine after that."

In the 1970s, the merger between Yarmouth and Dennis was hammered out, allowing the team to play at their current location, with a single team representing the Yarmouth-Dennis area. Longtime Y-D supporter and league official Don Tullie remembers the move:

"The Yarmouth team moved from Simkins Field on Route 28, across from the Yarmouth Town Hall over to Red Wilson Field. The reason Dennis came into the name was because, at that time, we used to get approximately $500 from the Dennis Recreation Department, and they demanded to be included in the activities. So they literally bought their name. So we had to, at that point, make them part of the name. It was a money issue. That's how the Yarmouth-Dennis Red Sox came into the league."

In 1984, a major insect problem destroyed the turf at the field and forced the Red Sox to play the majority of their home games at Whitehouse Field in Harwich. However, the field was reseeded in the off-season, and play resumed at Red Wilson Field the following year.

In the summer of 1986, Mike Bordick came to play for Yarmouth-Dennis. The middle infielder was a junior at Maine that spring, and had thoroughly expected to be drafted. He had a great year for a competitive Maine team, and it was hoped that his good defense, hustle, and a pretty fair bat would be enough for a shot at the majors.

But that first week in June, the chance that every youngster hopes for never came. Bordick was passed over. The undrafted free agent decided to head to Cape Cod. He was a New England guy, and heard that the Cape League was an excellent way to catch a scout's eye, and maybe make the majors that way.

"Well, he wasn't drafted," said Merrill "Red" Wilson, the Y-D coach that year. "But we had a centerfielder on our team that year from Princeton named Drew Stratton that Oakland had drafted in the 12th round, and Oakland kept talking to Drew through those few weeks about what they would offer him. You know, if you go to Princeton, you don't just sell your life for nothing."

The A's scout spent a lot of time around the Y-D club in the early days of that season. What he saw impressed him. But they were still interested in Stratton, who kept turning down the offers that Oakland was making. One night before the team was to head to Chatham, Stratton made his decision.

"Drew comes up to me before we leave," Wilson recalled. "He says 'Mr. Wilson, Oakland will be making me what I consider a final offer tonight. If I don't like it, I will turn it down and play for you the rest of the season.'

"I said I appreciated that, and we went to Chatham. Well, Drew had an average game that night, but Bordick made two plays in the field that were just major league. That night, Oakland signed Drew to a contract."

But the Oakland scout liked what he saw in Bordick. The next morning, he called Wilson and asked how to get in touch with Bordick. After speaking with Bordick, the scout phoned Oakland General Manager Sandy Alderson.

"What do you mean?" Alderson reportedly asked after the scout explained the situation.

"We can sign him for $25,000," replied the scout.

"Then get him," Alderson answered.

"I came home from a ballgame, and he was sitting on my back steps," said Barbara Ellsworth, who housed him. "He was still in uniform, and said 'We have to talk.' So we got in my car, and sat, and talked. He told me he had been made an offer, and he just didn't know what to do. I told him, as I tell all my players, 'I am in no position to tell you what to do, Michael.' That night, he called his folks. He agonized. He stayed upstairs that night, and he was awake most of the night. I could hear him, but I knew I should leave him alone."

"I got a call that night around 11 o'clock, and who was it, but Mike Bordick," said Wilson. "'Coach,' he said. 'I gotta tell you, Oakland made me an offer, and I'm going to sign tomorrow.' I wished him well, and he was gone the next day."

"He called constantly after he left," Ellsworth remembers. "He was only with us three weeks. But anything I've ever asked from him, he's delivered. He just never, ever, ever has forgotten from where he came.

"A few years later, I took four kids up to Fenway, and Michael was there, and we went back to the hotel so they could all rub elbows with the big shots. And when I was talking to someone, one of these kids leaned over and said to Michael 'Did she ever tell you not to forget from which you came?'

"And Michael leaned down and said, 'Why the hell do you think you're here?' That was pretty nice."

"I always tell that story because you never know who is watching you," Wilson said. "You might do something that will affect your future at any time, so always be your best. Three years after that, Drew is out of baseball, and Bordick is in the World Series."

The summer that Mike Bordick spent on the Cape was Red Wilson's last summer with Y-D. The longtime coach Wilson retired, and was replaced by the fiery Don Reed at the start of the 1987 campaign. The change was immediate.

"I was pretty laid-back," Wilson said in describing his coaching style. "Winning was never the most important thing with me as a coach. I tried to get as many players into the game as possible. I just read a quote from one of John Wooden's former players, who said that he never mentioned winning. He just talked about doing your best. I think I had that same sort of philosophy."

"Maybe it was because Don Reed came from a city atmosphere, but we started to get kids here who were from Pittsburgh, Detroit, and other big cities," Tullie said. "They were just tough, inner-city kids who were good baseball players. The whole atmosphere of hard-nosed baseball was created at Yarmouth under the direction of Don Reed. That was his style."

In 1989, Reed helped bring Y-D their first title, one of Don Tullie's favorite Cape League memories. Tullie has been a long-time Y-D supporter, as well as a former GM, and had worked as a league officer.

"1989 was the first time in 29 years that we won a championship," Tullie said. "We won it in the pouring rain, and I mean a downpour. And they gave Don Reed and me the championship trophy. I was so happy, I didn't even realize it was raining."

For Tullie, the '89 championship was the climax of much hard work that was needed to keep the Y-D franchise afloat throughout the 1970s.

"We go back to the days when we ran flea markets on Saturdays out of the old high school gym," said Tullie of himself and his wife. "We had to get every nickel and dime we could to keep this club afloat in the late '70s and into the '80s."

The present field as it looks today received its final finishing touches as late as 1992. In the early '90s, Y-D was one of the few remaining franchises without a press box and announcer's booth. That was remedied just prior to the 1991 season. But in August of that year Hurricane Bob, along with a nasty Halloween storm, had effectively destroyed both dugouts.

To remedy the situation, the Yarmouth-Dennis organization, along with the D-Y High baseball team, the Y-D Senior Babe Ruth, and the Cape Cod Titans of the American Legion, held a fund-raiser in mid-May. Players received pledges for the amount of innings, and spectators made donations at the games which helped raise enough money to ensure that the dugouts were ready for the summer of 1992.

Epilogue:
A Cape League Evening

It is a cool night in Orleans, Massachusetts, and in this coastal New England community, the summer day is winding slowly to a close. Breezes tease the American flag beyond the left field fence. While the afternoon brought the blazing heat and humidity of August, the cool evening reminds people that fall is not far behind.

The sun is setting beyond the horizon, and the people of the Lower Cape have come to enjoy some baseball. The parking lot fills quickly, and people bring their lawn chairs, sweatshirts, blankets and bug spray. They come to renew an age-old ritual, something that Cape Codders have done since the 1860s — watch baseball on Cape Cod.

Summertime on Cape Cod is magical enough, but Cape Cod baseball brings a sparkle to the eye of any New England baseball fan. It means summer afternoons lounging in the sun in Hyannis, or brisk evenings bundled up in a sweatshirt in Chatham. It means getting a first look at a hot young prospect named Frank Thomas or Carlton Fisk who suits up for Orleans, or getting an autograph from some college player named Jeff Bagwell from Chatham or Mo Vaughn from Wareham. But more than anything, it means developing relationships with players, people, and the game that has brought so much magic and joy.

Players toss the ball back and forth with the summertime laziness of little leaguers in the backyard having a catch. They are college baseball players, and many of them will be going on to the major leagues soon. But tonight, they are playing for their adoptive town. Whether it is Orleans, Chatham, or any of the eight other

225

teams on Cape Cod, they become part of the community. They work in the town during the day, and live with local families. They become as much a part of the town as the mailman or counter attendant at the community deli. And they develop relationships with the townsfolk that often last a lifetime.

On the grassy hillside, people mingle. Friends encounter friends. They renew old acquaintances, brought together by the game of baseball. They talk about family, about Cape Cod, but most of all, they talk baseball. Before the game, the National Anthem is played over the public-address system. Everybody takes off caps before the song begins, and sings along with the scratchy recording. They applaud happily when the song ends.

As the game continues, players turn in a spectacular brand of baseball. But the game is almost secondary to what is going on in the crowd. The hat is passed, and everyone gives a couple of dollars. Between innings, country or oldies music is played and little kids dance. Children chase foul balls, and are rewarded with free coupons for ice cream when they return them.

As the game continues, the only nastiness occurs when two young children fight over the same ice cream cone. Plays on both sides are cheered, and nobody boos when a ball is booted or a base is overthrown. And fans are close enough to the field that they can hear the infield chatter and smell the infield grass.

To get this close to a major league contest today, you would have to have either field level box seats or become a third-base coach. Here, the game is brought to you, in full color, surround sound, without the benefit of cable or pay-per-view television. And when a player slides head-first into third, you hear the umpire scream "Safe!" and see the runner hop up and dust himself off.

"The great thing about the Cape League is that you can get so close to the players," said Steve Buckley, columnist for the *Boston Herald* and ESPN2. "You are that much closer to them physically and emotionally. On a typical weeknight at a Cape League game you can get right up there and be a part of the game. But even more importantly, you're making an investment in the future of baseball. I've talked to more people who saw Frank Thomas play, and they'll remember it. And you're making an investment in the future of these players. And when they get to the big leagues, you say 'Omigod! I saw that guy in the Cape Cod League!' And that's kind of cool."

At the end of the game, everyone stands, dusts off and says "See you tomorrow!" as little kids run around the bases and ask players for their autographs.

There is a great sense of continuity here. The idea that your father and grandfather and great-grandfather sat on the same grassy hills and watched the same town teams floats through the cool night air. It is baseball caught in a time warp, taking you back to when baseball fans loved the game, without all the unnecessary trappings that would begin to surround the game and cloud the real meaning behind it. On Cape Cod, the game still remains sharply in focus for the fans, and that's what people come to see.

"The folksy atmosphere is what stands out for me," said Boston Red Sox GM Dan Duquette. "Being able to walk into a ballpark like Orleans and sit on a hill and watch a game. It's a great experience for the kids."

"In Chatham, you see the same families, year after year," said Russ Charpentier, who has covered the league for several area newspapers since the early '80s. "You see the same ones there all the time. Cotuit's the same way. And I'm sure that the kids today who run around chasing foul balls, I'm sure that it was their parents who were running around chasing foul balls when they were that age.

"Another thing that stands out in my mind is being [on the Cape] one night and watching a game with [major league scout] Lenny Merullo, and discovering that, not only did Lenny Merullo play in the Cape Cod League, but his son and grandson played in the Cape Cod League," Steve Buckley said. "That, to me, shows the time and the distance that the Cape Cod League has traveled."

On Cape Cod, people take away different things from the game and from the Cape Cod Baseball League in general. The player, whether he is the hottest college prospect in the nation or a fringe collegian looking for one last summer in the game he loves, takes away the possibility of making The Show, as well as a great summer in a terrific vacation community. But the fans take away something as well, maybe something even greater than the players. Sure, they get the memories of some great baseball, and maybe they can say that they gave a Jeff Bagwell a job washing dishes at their restaurant or Frank Thomas a job landscaping at their motel.

But more importantly, they have long-lasting friendships that develop with visiting players. Whether they meet them at a clinic or have one stay as a boarder at their house, they have the chance to get to know ballplayers.

"You see a guy like Ed Sprague, who every time he's in Boston, brings the family that put him up when he was in Cotuit to the game," said Peter Gammons of the *Boston Globe* and ESPN. "Mike Bordick too. These guys are very loyal to the families that they live with. The league brings in general managers for their hot-stove talks over the winter, but I'd like to see [them bring] some guys like Sprague, and maybe a couple of other guys, and explain what really makes this league special is not so much the baseball, but the relationships that develop between players and families."

"I stayed with the McCallisters, who were great," said Sprague. "But the people I stay in touch with the most are the Sadowskis, who help run the Cotuit team now. I met their kids in the clinic that we ran, and we've stayed in contact ever since. They follow us through the rest of our college career and our pro career. It's a great relationship. You get to meet some nice people that I still keep in contact with."

And the possibility of approaching a potential major league baseball player as a human being and not just a ballplayer helps bring the game into focus for people, and it helps humanize a sport that is in danger of being dehumanized completely.

No matter what conventional wisdom or nationwide polls tell us, there is still the unmistakable gleam in young people's eyes when they come into contact with the game of baseball. Whether it is through collecting cards, or recitation of statistics, or just getting an autograph, the memories a young person has of baseball are all good.

And those memories are reinforced through the work that many Cape Leaguers do at clinics. They teach the game to the youngsters, handing it down from generation to generation with care and delicacy. These players know how important the game is, and they bring a sense of the game's importance to these young people.

"Most personally rewarding for me was the opportunity I had to work with the kids in the [Orleans] Cardinals Baseball Clinic," said Florida Marlins outfielder Jeff Conie, who played in Orleans in 1986. "They got a lot out of it, sure, but it was a two-way street."

In the movie "Field of Dreams," there is an odd but happy co-incidence for fans of the Cape League. The young Archie "Moonlight" Graham is picked up by Ray Kinsella (Kevin Costner) and Terence Mann (James Earl Jones) as they are returning to Ray's farm in Iowa.

The young Archie breathlessly tells them he's a young ballplayer who's going to a place where they'll get you a job so you can "work during the day, and that'll let you play ball at night and on weekends." Ray laughs it off, saying they haven't done that kind of thing in years. What Ray didn't know was that Archie Graham was describing the Cape Cod Baseball League exactly.

In addition, an odd symmetry also occurs when Henry David Thoreau speaks of the Cape. He wrote, "At present it is wholly unknown to the fashionable world, and probably it will never be agreeable with them."

The Cape League has never been agreeable with the shifting sands of the outside game of baseball, and, until recently, was wholly unknown to the fashionable baseball universe. It has re-mained strong, true and defiant, like the fist of land that it imitates, standing firm against outside influences such as artificial turf, play-ers' strikes and free agency. The Cape League still remains true to the romantic ideal of the game of baseball — that it is simply a game, to be played with nine men on a side, four bases, three outs, and a village full of people cheering for both sides. And when it is played for the love of the game, it brings all kinds of people together.

Index

Page references in italics indicate illustration.

Other Books from On Cape Publications

Haunted Cape Cod & the Islands
by Mark Jasper
$14.95

Sea Stories of Cape Cod and the Islands
by Admont G. Clark
$39.95

Howie Schneider Unshucked:
A Cartoon Collection about the Cape, the Country and Life Itself
by Howie Schneider
$11.95

In the Footsteps of Thoreau:
25 Historic & Nature Walks on Cape Cod
by Adam Gamble
$14.95

Cape Cod
by Henry David Thoreau (Audio)
$19.95

Walking the Shores of Cape Cod
by Elliott Carr
$14.95

Cape Cod, Martha's Vineyard & Nantucket, the Geologic Story
by Robert N. Oldale
$14.95

1880 Atlas of Barnstable County:
Cape Cod's Earliest Atlas
$39.95

Quabbin:
A History & Explorer's Guide
by Michael Tougias
$18.95

On
Cape Publications

www.oncapepublications.com